Keeping Members

CEO Strategies for 21st Century Success

The
Myths
&
Realities

by Arlene Farber Sirkin and Michael P. McDermott

Foundation of the American Society of Association Executives

The authors have worked to ensure that all information in this book is accurate as of the time of publication and consistent with standards of good practice in the general management community. As research and practice advance, however, standards may change. For this reason it is recommended that readers evaluate the applicability of any recommendations in light of particular situations and changing standards.

Library of Congress Cataloging-in-Publication Data
Sirkin, Arlene Farber.
    Keeping members: the myths and realities/by Arlene Farber Sirkin and Michael McDermott.
        p. cm.
Includes bibliographical references (p.).
ISBN 0-88034-099-1
1. Trade and professional associations—United States—Membership.
2. Nonprofit organizations—United States—Membership.
3. Associations, institutions, etc.—United States—Membership.
4. Membership campaigns—United States. I. McDermott, Michael
(Michael P.) II. Title.
HD2425.S47 1995
061'.3'0688—dc20   95-34424
                                                     CIP

Foundation of the American Society of Association Executives
1575 Eye Street, N.W.
Washington, DC 20005-1168

Design by Design Consultants

Printed in the United States

*The ASAE Foundation
gratefully acknowledges
Seabury & Smith, Inc.,
insurance program managers,
for their generous sponsorship
of this project.*

Contents

Foreword

This project began with the assumption that members are the lifeblood of an association and that retaining those members through superior service is an association's core business. This statement may seem obvious enough. However, a review of the association management literature shows surprisingly little discussion about retaining members as a key strategic issue and organization-wide function. The dearth of comprehensive information in this area, and the vital nature of the topic to associations everywhere, led the ASAE Foundation to develop this study.

The in-depth research by authors Arlene Farber Sirkin and Michael McDermott involved more than 350 associations. The resulting practical book for developing a comprehensive, long-term retention strategy focuses on the importance of the CEO in leading an association staff effort to maximize member satisfaction and retention. In addition to its strategic guidance, this book offers practical and successful approaches for achieving this goal, including a strategic retention audit tool for diagnosing the current status of an association's retention efforts.

The ASAE Foundation is deeply indebted to Seabury & Smith, insurance program managers, for both their financial support and encouragement of this project. Their financial contribution to this project is but one of the many examples of how Seabury & Smith has, over the years, been a steadfast supporter and partner of the association community.

The ASAE Foundation Board is deeply grateful for the leadership and dedication of the ASAE Foundation Retention Task Force, chaired by James S. DeLizia, CAE. Task force members also included Mark Betchkal; Charles Deale, CAE; Robert Dolibois, CAE; Ann Oliveri; Harmon S. Pritchard, CAE; Jan Rickard; Thomas Schedler, CAE; and Pam Williams, CAE. Their thoughtful development and monitoring of this project has been critical to its success.

Collin C. Rorrie, Jr., Ph.D., CAE
Executive Director
American College of Emergency Physicians
1994-1995 Chair, ASAE Foundation

Acknowledgements

We owe a debt of gratitude to the hundreds of association executives who participated in our focus groups, survey research, one-on-one discussions, and site visits. Many of them generously shared their successes, failures, and experiences with us, either for attribution or anonymously. We appreciate the trust and confidence they showed in sharing information with us, with you, and with the profession. Likewise, we appreciate our past clients who gave us permission to quote from proprietary research, consulting, and seminars done with their members and staff.

Many of the positive examples come from a series of focus groups that we conducted with association executives. Because we promised anonymity to the participants, some of the examples are not attributed or use a generic description, such as "a national trade association."

This book reflects the efforts of many in addition to the authors. The ASAE Foundation Retention Task Force, headed by James DeLizia, CAE, guided the project. Ann Kenworthy, CAE, executive vice president and chief operating officer of the ASAE Foundation, provided staff direction. In addition, Allen Liff coordinated our work over the last year for the Foundation. Also deserving thanks are members of the ASAE Membership Section Council and the ASAE publishing staff, especially Linda Munday and Elissa M. Myers, CAE.

We also wish to thank the following individuals for their special contribution to this book: Trudy Aron; Judith A. Barnes; Roger S. Beadle; Gene S. Bergoffen, CAE; Paul E. Borawski; Irma Brosseau; Donna G. Childs; Garis F. Distelhorst, CAE; Thomas C. Dolan, Ph.D., CAE; Richard F. Dorman, CAE; Brenda C. Dost, CAE; Henry L. Ernstthal, CAE; Mary Beth Fidler; Thomas A. Gorski, CAE; Mary Jane Kolar, CAE; Molly Maguire; Ralph J. Marlatt, CAE; Janet McCallen, CAE; Ginger Nichols, CAE; Robert V. Piemonte, Ed.D., CAE; Harmon O. Pritchard, Jr., CAE; Jeffry W. Raynes, CAE; Rick E. Russell; Susan Sarfati, CAE; Jay L. Schiavo, CAE; Debra Sher; Patricia A. Siegel, CAE; The ASAE Membership Marketing Council; Holley Urbanski; and Patricia K. Wood.

A special thanks goes to Seabury & Smith, which had the foresight to support the profession by funding this project of the ASAE Foundation.

For their gifts of time and support, we want to thank Chris McDermott, Stella Mendoza, and Joshua and Stuart Sirkin.

We hope that this will be the first in a series of publications focusing on strategic membership retention. The topic is of paramount importance to the continued growth and success of associations and other membership-based organizations.

Arlene Farber Sirkin   Washington, D.C.

Michael P. McDermott   August 1995

Special thanks to the following associations for providing examples of membership-related programs and services:

American Academy of Family Physicians
Kansas City, Missouri

American Association of Retired Persons
Washington, D.C.

American Bankers Association
Washington, D.C.

American Ceramic Society
Westerville, Ohio

American Chamber of Commerce Executives
Alexandria, Virginia

American College of Health Care Administrators
Alexandria, Virginia

American Dental Association
Chicago, Illinois

American Immigration Lawyers Association
Washington, D.C.

American Library Association
Chicago, Illinois

American Marketing Association
New York, New York

American Society for Quality Control
Milwaukee, Wisconsin

American Society of Corporate Secretaries
New York, New York

American Society of Mechanical Engineers
New York, New York

Association for Corporate Computing Technical Professionals
Greenfield, Wisconsin

B'nai Brith Women
Washington, D.C.

Building Owners and Managers Association International
Washington, D.C.

Footwear Industries of America
Washington, D.C.

Grand Rapids Home Builders Association
Grand Rapids, Michigan

International Map Trade Association
Kankakee, Illinois

League of Women Voters
Washington, D.C.

Michigan Manufacturers Association
Lansing, Michigan

Mothers Against Drunk Driving
Irving, Texas

National Association of College Stores
Oberlin, Ohio

National Association of Home Builders
Washington, D.C.

National Association of Life Underwriters
Washington, D.C.

National Association of Professional Insurance Agents
Alexandria, Virginia

National Cattlemen's Association
Englewood, Colorado

National Speakers Association
Tempe, Arizona

Optical Society of America
Washington, D.C.

Pittsburgh High Technology Council
Pittsburgh, Pennsylvania

Society for Foodservice Management
Louisville, Kentucky

About the Authors

Arlene Farber Sirkin is a nationally recognized speaker, writer, and consultant in the areas of membership, marketing, and leadership. Since 1989 she has been president of the Washington Resource Consulting Group, Inc. (WRCG), a firm that works with associations and other membership organizations to help them maximize their members/customers through consulting, research, and training. WRCG is a leader in the area of strategic retention audits, including member and product evaluation and development.

Ms. Sirkin has taught on the faculty of several universities and in a number of ongoing programs for association and chamber executives such as the U.S. Chamber of Commerce's Institute for Organization Management. Ms. Sirkin received the Monument Award from the Greater Washington Society of Association Executives and has been named to the Keynoters on Tour program of the American Marketing Association. She holds a master's degree from Columbia University and an MBA from Wharton.

Michael P. McDermott is a freelance writer with an expertise in nonprofit marketing. He has developed and conducted more than 50 seminars and has published numerous articles and papers in this area. He has had a broad range of membership experience at the local, national, and international level of both trade and professional associations. His involvement with associations extends to active participation as a volunteer, including chapter president, Global Marketing Division vice president, and national board member of the American Marketing Association and board vice president of the International Map Trade Association. Mr. McDermott has a master's degree in writing from George Mason University.

Introduction

For years some associations have based their retention efforts on myths such as "The membership department handles retention" and "All members are the same." This book puts those and other myths to rest. By focusing on the *realities* of retention, *Keeping Members* shows how associations can maximize members' satisfaction, membership retention, and the bottom line.

Management guru Peter Drucker poses three basic questions to organizations: What is our business? Who is our customer? What does the customer consider value? The association that can answer these questions has taken the first step toward a successful retention strategy.

What members value will change over time, and so must membership benefits—the products and services, both tangible and intangible, that the association delivers. In this way, the association continues to create the value that turns members into lifetime customers.

Membership retention works best as a strategic process woven into the day-to-day operations of the association. That means it requires the attention of everyone, from staff members as well as volunteers. And as with any other strategic initiative, membership retention is an effort most effectively led by the chief staff officer (referred to in this book as the CEO). In the absence of a paid staff, the chief elected officer or highest-ranking volunteer usually fills this role.

Many associations are also observing that members are less likely to renew simply because "we've always belonged." With members continually evaluating the value they receive in return for their dues checks, the membership retention process clearly ties in with every other strategic initiative undertaken by an association.

Granted, no one set of rules applies to membership retention, which by definition needs to be customized to the members of each association. Some associations have individuals as members, others have companies or organizations as members, and a few have both. Still, some basic principles apply to all membership organizations. Those principles—or realities—are what this book is about.

Overview of the Contents

Research for this book started with literature searches for existing information on membership retention and related topics. We then conducted original research with hundreds of association CEOs and executives using focus groups, surveys, and one-on-one interviews and site visits. We also used proprietary research that we had done for clients (with their permission), as well as proprietary research that some associations generously shared with us to further the efforts of the project, the foundation, and the profession.

This book examines how associations can implement membership retention as a critical strategic process—what we refer to as *strategic retention*. Because of this perspective, none of the chapters covers how-to details, such as the components of a renewal mailing. Rather, each chapter looks at a particular principle or approach that you can take to ensure you're integrating membership retention into other strategic processes. For instance, the book highlights the rapidly changing business and communications environment and its effect on association members, how to determine what your members need today, and how to communicate with your members from their own perspective.

The bottom line is the need for practical strategic leadership by the CEO. With your leadership, membership retention can be the key to your association's success in the 21st century.

Ways to Use This Book

Although this book is aimed at association CEOs, it can also serve as a guide for addressing strategic retention issues among all segments of your organization.

Given the variety of learning styles and levels of membership expertise among association executives, we've provided multiple ways of accessing the information in this book. We encourage you to read Chapter 1 so you understand the approach and context of the book. Then, if you're in a rush, refer to the key points of information that are graphically highlighted throughout the text.

To help you translate the theories into practice, the book concludes with an Association Strategic Retention Audit (See Chapter 11). This formal analytical tool, designed to help you evaluate your retention efforts, can be used in your association. Although the audit primarily focuses on strategic concerns, it also raises issues that will have tactical and operational implications for your association's retention efforts.

Chapter 1

Membership Retention— The Ultimate Bottom Line

As a global economy emerges, the information highway takes shape, and managerial hierarchies fade away in favor of flatter organizations, associations and their members can't help but be affected. Because of major advances in communications and computer technology, the effects of world trends are now felt immediately by the individuals as well as the corporations that belong to membership organizations. Consider, for instance, the following situations:

- Suppose the major companies within your industry or profession decided that they could do the same work at a fraction of the cost by relocating to another country. If they followed through on the plan, what might happen to the membership of your organization?

- If your members could gather all the information they needed from databases located all over the world—without ever contacting your association—why would they need to remain a member?

- Imagine what might happen to your retention rate if many of your members in middle management were "rightsized" right out of their jobs.

"Retention is even more important than recruitment. You can always get new people into the fold, but keeping them is the real challenge. You have to be an evolving association, keeping on top of the wants and needs of the members."

—*Trudy Aron, executive director, Kansas State Chapter, American Institute of Architects, Topeka*

These represent just a few of the gut-wrenching, can't-sleep-at-night scenarios that plague association executives as they face the inevitability of change along with the arrival of the 21st century. Membership retention offers an important indicator of how well the organization is responding to these changes. In addition, when approached strategically, retention connects associations to the realities of the changing world.

A Revolution of Changes

In a *Fortune* magazine article entitled "Welcome to the Revolution," Thomas A. Stewart examines the changes sweeping the world and categorizes them into four simultaneous revolutions. Each one directly affects the other three. Let's look at the four revolutions in the context of member retention:

1. **Globalization of markets.** Retention is the measure of the relative value that membership organizations offer; members will stay if they believe their associations can help them succeed in the changing marketplace. At the same time, organizations that can change with their current members—wherever they are or wherever they do business—will survive and prosper in the global economy.

2. **Spread of information technology and computer networks.** This revolution has an almost ironic effect because the lifeblood of any membership organization is its ability to communicate with members as well as facilitate communication between members. If members can access information and contact one another via electronic means, why should they pay dues to receive an association's monthly publication and attend its annual conference? Associations that can answer that question or adapt to that change have a much better chance of retaining members.

3. **Dismantling of hierarchial management.** The "flattening" of corporate America into more horizontal structures could have devastating consequences. Many associations still reflect the once predominant hierarchial structure within their own memberships and structures. For example, some professional memberships are based on job function—if that function ceases to exist, the association may disappear as well.

4. **New information-age economy.** Societies throughout the world now value knowledge and quick communication more than physical labor and natural resources. On the plus side, the majority of goods and services offered by membership organizations are already information-based. But are they communicating the information in the right way?

Remaining Relevant

Members don't exist in a vacuum, but rather in a constantly changing world. You need to know what your members value about their membership and how your members' needs are changing to be able to respond in a meaningful way; if you cannot respond, some other membership organization or for-profit group will be ready to fulfill those unmet needs.

Clearly, retention is a fundamental measure of how relevant the association is to your members. If you don't offer what they need—if there's no value relative to belonging to your organization—they'll vote with their feet and leave.

Researchers in customer satisfaction have estimated that you'll spend between five and 15 times more to recruit a new customer (member) than to keep an existing one. Similar numbers probably apply to association members. Retention has become an economic necessity and, therefore, a strategic survival and growth issue for all membership organizations.

myth 1

The membership department handles retention.

reality

The CEO sets the tone and ensures that retention becomes and remains a key strategic focus for the entire organization. Although the membership department may develop and spearhead member services, strategic retention is everybody's job, staff as well as volunteers.

Without members, an association has little or no reason to exist. With members who continue to make the decision to renew, an association has a good measure of its success. Retention directly affects the bottom line. It pays your salary and can mean the difference between being the CEO of a thriving organization or the CEO of a shrinking entity—all the more reason for you to take the lead in emphasizing the importance of retention to your association.

Myths Versus Realities

Sadly, too many association CEOs pay attention to retention when it is too late—when a noticeable number of members have left. That may be because they're influenced by membership retention myths that have taken hold over the years and become common wisdom.

The first step in understanding retention as a strategic process is to dispel those myths and replace them with retention realities that emphasize the CEO's leadership role. Look at the 12 statements below and decide whether they are retention myths or realities.

	Myth	Reality
1. The membership department handles retention.	_____	_____
2. Retention equals renewal.	_____	_____
3. Recruitment and retention get equal resources.	_____	_____
4. There are always more new members to recruit.	_____	_____
5. There is one ideal retention rate.	_____	_____
6. High nondues revenues eliminate retention worries.	_____	_____
7. Our members will renew no matter what we do.	_____	_____
8. The staff knows what our members want.	_____	_____
9. A "golden handcuff" means a captive audience.	_____	_____
10. All members are the same.	_____	_____
11. Just send the new member a kit.	_____	_____
12. Retention begins the moment a member joins.	_____	_____

Some may find this hard to believe, but all 12 of the statements above have been found to be retention myths. On the next page you'll find a chart of the 12 retention myths and their accompanying realities, plus a reference to the chapter in which each is addressed. The chart outlines this book's discussion of the concepts and strategies that will provide the key to the survival and growth of any association in the 21st century.

Retention Myths v. Realities

Retention Myth	Retention Reality	Chapter
1. The membership department handles retention.	The CEO must emphasize the priority of retention and set the tone for the staff and volunteers.	1
2. Retention equals renewal.	Renewal is only the last step in the long process of retention.	2
3. Recruitment and retention get equal resources.	Many associations give the lion's share of resources to recruitment.	2
4. There are always more new members to recruit.	For growth to occur, two members must be recruited to replace one lost member. When a member is retained, growth occurs with each new recruit.	2
5. There is one ideal retention rate.	Retention is a complex process affected by various forces. It is unique to each association.	3
6. High nondues revenues eliminate retention worries.	Members form the primary customer base for most associations; to lose members is to lose customers.	4
7. Our members will renew no matter what we do.	Members continually evaluate the value of their membership. To keep members, associations must "deliver the goods."	4
8. The staff knows what our members want.	A good staff knows about its members, but only from a staff perspective. Research provides the member perspective.	5
9. A "golden handcuff" means a captive audience.	The best "lock" on members is to be indispensable by responding to their needs.	5
10. All members are the same.	Maximizing retention requires treating each member as an individual.	8
11. Just send the new member a kit.	Paying special attention to first-year members can convert them into active lifetime members.	9
12. Retention begins the moment a member joins.	Retention is tied in part to how a member was recruited; it starts with the first contact, even before joining.	9

Chapter 2

The Core Issues of Strategic Retention

W hen we asked 100 association CEOs to define retention, we heard a wide range of responses. Several defined it as the clerical function of processing renewals, while others viewed it as sending out X notices over the course of Y months. Others defined it as a number, as in "We have 85 percent retention." Many seemed surprised at the question because the definition is obvious: Retention refers to the people who were members last year who paid their dues on time this year.

In addition to asking that question while preparing this book, we asked hundreds of association executives to identify other organizations that had successful retention processes in place. Whether they were at the national, state, or local level, almost all said they couldn't identify any associations with full and effective retention programs.

What Is Strategic Retention?

Perhaps these executives had difficulty answering the question because the association community doesn't have an accepted definition for retention. This book proposes one:

Membership retention is the strategic integrated process implemented daily by the association CEO, staff, and volunteers that creates or delivers sufficient perceived value to result in member renewal.

Based on this definition, a shorthand way to describe the process is "strategic retention." If implemented daily at all levels of your association, strategic retention includes many pieces, which all add up to a member's perception of value. Members, for instance, base their perception on their interactions with staff and leaders, your association's products and services, and the information and opportunities provided (including networking with other members). They determine whether they've received enough value from the interactions, the products, and the information to be satisfied—to make retaining membership worth their efforts and expenditures.

In other words, strategic retention results from integrated and association-wide efforts. That's why the retention process must involve everyone—the volunteers as well as the staff members who deliver products and services every day in the effort to meet members' needs. Your association may have recognized years ago that the strategic retention process is the key to your future existence and success. However, if you've come to that realization recently, improving the strategic retention process may require significant restructuring of your association.

myth 2

Retention equals renewal.

reality

Renewal is only the last step in the long process of retention. Members pay their dues again if they are satisfied and feel they have received value throughout the year.

As the CEO you must not only initiate this effort but also lead it. In addition to setting the tone for retention efforts, you need a clearly defined strategic vision for making member satisfaction and retention a priority for all staff and volunteers. Strategic retention is everyone's job.

Delivering the Goods

Is retention a managerial or clerical function? If you believe the latter—that the retention process primarily is invoicing, mailing cycles, and anniversary dates—you may not be particularly concerned as long as the "retention rate" does not fall below a certain number.

In fact, retention has elements of both functions. The CEO ensures that retention efforts permeate every part of the association; otherwise, retention becomes nothing more than a computer program. Yet for the association to have the funds to exist, the invoices must be mailed and the dues checks deposited. Retention is a symbiotic relationship, with one function depending on the other.

At the Heart of the Matter

If you're still holding on to Myth #2—that the clerical task of renewal equals retention—think about the difference between meeting registration and the meeting planning process.

Registration is an administrative piece of the entire process. It is an important function, but members don't base their decision on whether to attend a meeting on how well the registration form is designed or how early it's mailed. Instead, they consider many factors, including programming, location, cost, promotional materials, and so forth. If meeting attendance is down, improving the registration procedures will not solve the core problem.

Likewise, renewal is an administrative part of the entire retention process. It's certainly a visible part, but it's not at the core of the issue. If your association has low retention, improving renewal procedures will not solve the underlying problem.

Both the managerial and clerical functions combine in pursuit of the same goal: delivering the goods. This means continually providing benefits, communicating those benefits, meeting and exceeding expectations, knowing and being flexible enough to meet members' needs, involving members wherever possible, and guaranteeing their satisfaction.

While elected leaders may establish the organizational vision, the CEO must ensure that it gets implemented. The entire staff and volunteers must translate that vision into the goods and services that members want, need, and value. In multi-level membership organizations, such as those with state, regional, or international chapters, the translation must ring true with the values of the local affiliates. Strategic retention is hard work because it requires delivering on the promise, fulfilling the order, and satisfying the customer.

One Association's Vision

As an example of how you can make member satisfaction a priority for everyone, here's the vision that guides staff of the National Association of College Stores:

We will become indispensable to our members through service excellence and a commitment to listening and responding with personalized, caring service to them and to one another.

• Members/customers are the sole basis and justification of our existence, and our responsiveness, flexibility, services, and attitude must be overly sensitive to their needs.

• Our association succeeds through its people, and our people will commit themselves to the association's vision and to unselfish teamwork while striving to achieve personal performance levels that go beyond the standard.

• We are an organization that cares—for our members and for each other. We will treat one another with respect and with a caring attitude knowing that our collective value is the key to our total success.

• Innovation and risk taking are promoted and fostered from within by encouraging our people to be active in the development and implementation of ideas that will make NACS Inc. a stronger organization.

• We administer our responsibilities with professionalism and by leadership example for all to see.

• We are a financially sound organization and will maintain this position by adhering to a philosophy of conservative, but realistic, financial planning and careful management of our assets.

Sibling Rivalry

You'd be hard-pressed to pick up any article or book on association membership and not see the words *recruitment* and *retention* coupled together. According to conventional wisdom, the two go hand-in-hand—they're equal partners. But a closer look reveals anything but a true partnership.

The majority of membership-related literature, for example, devotes the most space to recruitment. After examining the recruitment process in microscopic detail, many articles discuss retention in the last few pages. In many associations, recruitment gets more resources, more money, more time, and more emphasis overall. These situations reflect the sad reality of the sibling rivalry between these traditional components of membership. Recruitment is the big brother, attracting all the attention and family finances. Retention is often the poor stepsister, getting the hand-me-downs and left-overs.

Why is this? In theory, many associations assign the same staff members to both recruitment and retention. In practice, however, staff members expend the majority of their effort (time) and resources (money) on bringing in new members. Ask your membership department to assign percentages of the time they spend on recruitment versus retention; you may be surprised at the disparity.

myth 3

Recruitment and retention get equal resources.

reality

Many associations give the lion's share of resources (time and money) to recruiting new members. Recruitment shows short-term payback, while retention is a long-term strategy that requires hard work. In the long term, however, emphasizing retention is the wisest investment your association can make.

Focusing on recruitment has the advantage of showing a quick economic return—bringing in new members is viewed as more profitable because it translates into instant cash flow. Also, it's often easier to see a direct cause-and-effect relationship with recruitment: "If I spend X dollars on recruitment, I know I'll bring in Y new members, who will bring in Z new dollars

Recruiting For 1 year

for the association.' ... ı as the front end of the
retention process. ... asteful and expensive
mistake for associat ... d often the only opportunity you may ha ... ember. You need to be
recruiting for reten....

Slowing the Outward Flow

Until recently, many industries, professions, and organizations operated in a
growth mode. Associations often could pay little attention to the members
leaving through the back door because plenty more kept coming in the front door. A former president of a large chapter of the American Marketing Association, for example, remembers that the chapter didn't even address retention during the 1980s because it was so busy handling the influx of new members.

*There are always more new
members to recruit.*

*When you lose a member, you must
recruit two in order to show
growth. When you retain a member,
however, growth occurs with every
new recruit. Most associations
have a limited pool of prospects
that's often narrowly defined.
Money is much better spent keeping
the members you have rather than
locating possible new recruits, some
of which will never join no matter
what you do.*

Some associations act as if they have unlimited new prospects. But what happens when people stop knocking on the front door? If that back door is still open, you'll be left with an empty house.

The term to describe this in-and-out flow of members is churn. To use another analogy, think of a bucket filled with sand but with a small hole in the bottom. To keep the sand at the same level, you'd have to refill the bucket constantly to keep pace with what's flowing out. That's churn. That's also an expensive, time-consuming, and risky approach when it comes to membership. You spend your resources filling the pail (recruitment), then repeat the same procedures and expenditures to replace what's fallen out the bottom (recruitment again).

Now think of how much easier it would be to keep the bucket full of sand if you reduced the size of the hole or, better yet, plugged the hole completely (retention). Even a small reduction in the size of the hole could free you up to do something other than shovel in more sand.

Your association loses heavily from a lapsed member. Gone are the lifetime income and volunteer support that member could have generated. Only after your association has replaced its membership losses can it begin to grow. What might be the implications of reducing your annual loss by 1 percent, 5 percent, or even 10 percent? Chances are, you'd see an immediate growth in the size of the association and its revenues. If you take into account the lifetime income and value of each member, you're talking about a lot of members and potential revenue. Not closing the hole through strategic retention is like leaving money on the table. It is a missed opportunity, one that's very expensive for your association.

Churn can also increase member dissatisfaction. A dissatisfied ex-member may discourage prospects from joining or even persuade others from renewing. As has been widely reported, dissatisfied customers are more likely to tell others of their bad experience than satisfied customers are to tell of their good experience.

Ironically, even if you equalize your retention and recruitment efforts, you are not doing enough. For the best results, you need to put far more effort and resources into retention, into stopping the flow of sand out of the bottom of the pail. **Retention is the best method to protect your association's "pot of gold"—the current members.**

Retention Starts With Recruitment

The strategic retention of a member begins the day the recruitment process begins. How the association recruits and who does the recruiting can affect retention. For example, some associations have found that members recruited by other members have a higher retention rate than those recruited through direct mail. You need to determine which recruitment methods are most effective for your association, based on your past history, research, and membership.

Whether the point of initial contact is a volunteer, a staff person, or even a direct mail piece, every succeeding interaction between your association and the prospect affects retention. As the National Association of Home Builders says in its *Playing for Keeps: Retention Handbook*: "Don't just focus on getting the check, but on gaining a member who is interested and committed to the association. When planning a membership drive, the ultimate goal should be to recruit members who will remain members for more than one year."

Sometimes a well-meaning but ill-informed volunteer trying to win a member-get-a-member campaign, or a staff person or third-party telemarketer trying to meet a quota, can set up your association for retention failure. To avoid being sabotaged by false promises made to prospects, recruiters must create realistic expectations for the members they are recruiting. Developing effective recruiting materials, including brochures, telemarketing scripts, and videos, helps ensure realistic expectations. Some associations have instituted training programs that emphasize recruiting "for keeps."

> **❝Retention starts with the CEO. We are a small business, and members are our customers. They give us our paychecks, a fact that emphasizes the importance of members to our survival.❞**
>
> —*Gene Bergoffen, CAE, executive vice president, National Private Truck Council*

The costs of servicing a new member, such as providing a welcome kit and setting up a computer file, are often higher for a first-year member. As a result, churn in the new-member category becomes particularly expensive. If you have a limited pool of qualified prospective members, you may only get one shot at recruiting for retention. It is too expensive an opportunity to waste.

If the people responsible for recruiting new members have an incentive to make sure their recruits renew, retention will often increase. For instance, some associations have reduced churn by tying recruitment campaigns to retention requirements or bonuses. One association executive, writing in the ASAE *Membership Marketer*, spoke for many when she noted, "Retention, the flip side of recruitment, is hard work. It's not as much fun or as exciting, and people tend not to spend as much time doing it . . . . There's a tendency to say, 'I brought them in—it's up to the society to keep them in.'"

It's not so much a matter of hard work that differentiates recruitment from retention. Anyone who has ever implemented a full-scale recruitment program, complete with phonathon, flights of direct mail, and follow-ups that never seem to end, certainly has a right to say that recruitment isn't easy. The difference is that recruitment has a clear and distinct end. It's finished when the prospect becomes a member or turns you down. Recruitment has a short-term, finite focus and often produces immediate results in the form of new members and dues dollars.

In contrast, retention never ends. The work comes in countless different ways, from spelling the member's name right, to tracking the last time a member did something for or bought something from the organization, to thanking the member for renewing. What may seem like minutiae or administrative trivia are nevertheless important to members. As a CEO of a regional trade association says, "My members are CEOs, and we find that they judge us by the small things. If we can't get the telephones answered in a timely way or the mail out correctly, how can they trust us with their lobbying and legislative efforts?"

Another CEO, a female executive director whose first name is Michael, tells of her frustration in receiving mail addressed to 'Mr.' "It's bad enough when it is junk mail from a vendor who I don't know, trying to sell me things I don't want. But I belonged to a professional association. I paid them my money to be put on their mailing list, and they couldn't get it right! I called twice, and the next time it happened I dropped my membership. When we get a new member we call to verify all information. We get it right the first time so it is right from the start."

Your association exists to respond to its members and to serve their needs. From the moment a prospect has contact with your organization, whether via a phone call or by attending an event, the hard work of strategic retention begins.

What's a Member Worth?

Since the late 1970s, determining member worth has gone through a significant evolution.

Traditionally, associations calculated the monetary value of a member by the amount of annual dues. The more dues paid, the more valuable, economically speaking, was the member. The next step was looking at the member's purchases of products and services. As these purchases became a growing factor in the income stream of most associations, they were aggregated into a lump sum and usually called non-dues revenues.

More recently, a member's monetary value has been looked at from the perspective of what he or she contributes while remaining a member—what's known as lifetime value. True lifetime value not only examines the income but also the costs (direct and indirect, fixed and variable) of obtaining and servicing the member. Economies of scale also come into play as membership numbers increase.

Lifetime value also includes the non-economic contribution of volunteer efforts—the hundreds and thousands of hours of free services that members donate by being active in the association. Many of the most successful programs and even the management of some associations depend on these volunteer services, which are often never counted or quantified. If you added up the value of these hours of contributed services, you'd probably find the total substantial, even using an artificially low figure, such as minimum wage, for the calculation. Likewise, many associations find that the majority of new members who retain their membership were recruited by existing members. In that case, the economic value of a member who is an effective recruiter is increased by a significant multiplier.

Considering both the economic and non-economic contributions of members helps to focus on the long-term value of a member and the importance of investing in retention. For example, you can use lifetime value to justify investment in research about what members want or to emphasize to staff how valuable each member is to the association.

The Cachet of Membership

Since the early 1990s, corporate America has shifted its emphasis from obtaining new customers to retaining current customers. This shift is not for altruistic reasons. Corporations do it because it is good business.

Consider the frequent flyer programs and clubs introduced by virtually every airline. Retention is the motivation behind their talk of customer loyalty, customer relations, and building customer relationships. Hotels, magazines, credit-card companies, and retailers have followed suit in seeking ways to cement a long-term relationship with their existing customers. They've invested in research, databases, and customer-service programs in a long-term strategy that requires time and resources.

Calculating Lifetime Income

How much does one member contribute to your association's bottom line? By looking at one year's dues, you see only a small part of a member's economic value. But by looking at retention patterns, you can calculate the average length of membership. Once you've established that number, you can calculate a simplified lifetime income: Add the average dues to the average non-dues revenue and multiply the resulting sum by the average number of years of membership.

Assume, for example, that dues average $100 per year, nondues income averages $75 per year, and the average length of membership is 10 years. Lifetime income would equal ($100 + $75) X 10 or $1,750. If the average length of membership were 20 years, lifetime income would equal ($100 + $75) X 20 or $3,500.

You'll immediately see the financial returns of a good retention plan. Granted, you'll have to balance lifetime income against costs to recruit and service a member, as well as discounting the flow of future income to its present value.

Many of these programs use the term "member" or "membership" because it appears to have a cachet of loyalty from the individual customer. American Express, for example, has used the slogan "Membership has its privileges." The idea of becoming a member—as opposed to a customer, user, or subscriber—is becoming more pervasive. Your mail might contain an offer to buy a membership to a series of concerts or theater events; a local mall might make you a member of its shoppers club if you spend X amount of dollars at its stores.

Obviously, associations have a big advantage over the commercial sector—they start with this membership cachet as their foundation. It is a valuable asset that needs to be protected. When you have an effective retention process, you enhance the cachet of membership in your association and the benefits of membership.

Chapter 3

What's In A Number?

To gauge the success of their efforts to provide value to members, associations generally use two measurements: the *attrition rate* and the *retention rate*. Attrition, also known as turnover, refers to the number or percentage of members lost during a given period, usually a fiscal or calendar year. On the other side of the membership coin, retention refers to the number or percentage of members who retain their membership in the association.

Of the two, the retention rate is reported most often because it accents the positive—the members kept rather than the members lost. Neither rate, however, is inherently better than the other as a basic membership figure. In some instances, you may decide to present the attrition figure because it's usually the smaller of the two. In other instances, perhaps when you want to demonstrate significant growth or the success of a membership program, you might want to use the typically larger retention figure. For consistency, this book discusses the more prevalent retention rate.

As an association, however, focusing solely on retention rates can be harmful. For instance, problems have been reported when volunteer presidents or other elected leaders arbitrarily raise the target retention rate for *their* term in office. One CEO of a local individual membership organization describes what can happen: "Our president decided that our retention rate was too low, so we mounted an aggressive member-keep-a-member campaign with some exciting prizes. But he did not want to 'waste' time or money to provide materials or to train the volunteers as we had in the past. Some of our overly enthusiastic volunteers made unrealistic promises. We even found one volunteer actually had subsidized someone's dues to win a prize.

"The president also insisted that we increase the length of time that we counted lapsed members as retained. (We did, however, draw the line when he wanted us to count the membership dues that had not been paid—from members who had not indicated they planned to renew—as accounts receivable.) The result was that we met the goals for *his* year, but our attrition the next year was higher than ever before."

Making the Correct Calculations

Attrition, or turnover, refers to the percentage of members lost during a given period, usually a fiscal or calendar year. In simple terms, the attrition, turnover, or loss rate equals the total number of members not retained divided by the total number of members in the previous year.

For example, if your association lost 100 members out of the previous year's total membership of 1,000, its attrition or turnover rate would be 10 percent [100 ÷ 1,000 = 10%].

Conversely, a retention rate measures the number of members kept during a given period, usually a fiscal or calendar year. The formula is: Total Number of Members Retained ÷ Total Number of Members in Previous Year.

Using the example above, your association kept 900 members out of the previous year's total of 1,000. The retention rate would be 90 percent [900 ÷ 1,000 = 90%]. Another way of looking at it is: 100% – Attrition Rate = Retention Rate (in the example used above, the calculation would be 100% – 10% = 90%).

Timing—when during the year you calculate the retention rate—can significantly affect the resulting figure. Even if your association doesn't have an annual renewal date, you may still see a surge of renewals at selected times of the year. Calculating the retention rate before those times or the annual renewal date will make it look much better than the same measurement three months later. By manipulating timing and assumptions, such as figuring that all members who have not yet paid will still renew, you can influence the retention rate—but only for the short-term.

A few associations determine retention rates by counting bodies rather than specific members. For instance, if their association had 1,000 members on January 1, 1995, and 1,000 members on January 2, 1996, they might say they had a 100-percent retention rate even though 250 of the members in 1996 were different people than in 1995. In contrast, typically most associations would say they had a 75-percent retention rate and a 25-percent attrition or turnover rate. They'd also indicate that new members represent 25 percent of their current membership. This gives a more accurate picture of what is happening and is an industry-wide trend.

Taking the Long View

As noted in the example above, membership fall-off can often be traced to using retention (and recruiting) tactics that aren't in the long-term interest of the association and its members. For a long-range perspective, use retention rates as a strategic tool in the following ways:

• **Evaluate historical trends.** Although your current retention rate helps you evaluate what's happening with membership today, looking at the association's history can help you identify and understand changes that have shaped the association along the way. Review retention rates for the last five to 10 years and identify any factors that might have significantly influenced retention for each year.

For example, did the industry experience a wave of mergers and acquisitions, or did the profession witness a large number of people retiring? The economy in general may have prompted large-scale downsizing within an industry or profession, which in turn put pressures on your association to downsize in response to members' situations. Or perhaps your retention rates have steadily increased because of demographic or economic factors.

Analyze each factor to determine if it is an isolated incident or part of a trend. This information can be helpful in identifying ways to support an increasing retention rate or to slow a decreasing retention rate. Sometimes, as in the case of a mature industry undergoing mergers and acquisitions, there's no way to increase the retention rate. If you've identified the start of a downward trend, your association will need to reexamine the effects on its operation, especially its dues structure, and consider redefining its market.

By using the retention rate to look at the past as compared to the present and future, you'll get a good picture of what's been going on with membership overall. Identifying and understanding significant changes will help you set realistic targets for the next year's retention rate.

• **Target member segments.** Even if your association doesn't have formalized special-interest groups (See Chapter 8), identify specific segments or markets that present a higher risk for members not renewing. These groups may be based on factors such as length of membership (new members), geography (members of a particular chapter), function, demographics, or use of a particular product or service (which may be unsatisfactory). Many of the groups with the highest retention risk do not fall into typical association membership categories (such as students or vendors) that are most frequently analyzed for retention risk. Identifying the correct, often "hidden," groups most at risk can be a difficult but necessary exercise. Then, through research, identify what is necessary to get more members in these specific groups to value and consequently retain their membership.

Some associations, for example, have found that the more senior members often drop their membership after reaching a certain professional level or years of experience. They may feel the programs weren't advanced enough or didn't provide the right industry contacts. In response, some associations have created advanced programming, special benefits aimed at senior members, and new volunteer opportunities such as mentoring and advisory programs. This is an example of a hidden group that is likely to be overlooked.

In view of high attrition rates, other associations have targeted graduating student members. Accustomed to paying an artificially low student rate, recent graduates can be highly sensitive to price and resent getting hit with the regular (and higher) dues rate just as they're starting a job. Some associations have responded by introducing lower-cost "bridge" memberships for those just out of school, with gradual dues increases occurring annually for up to five years. Alumni associations often use this approach, too.

If you have a membership category for vendors who want to market to your core membership (often called associate or affiliate members), you may notice lower retention rates in this category compared to the association overall. In some cases, vendors or suppliers believe they're treated as second-class citizens; in others, they have unrealistic expectations as to how the association will generate business contacts and opportunities for them.

The hardest part is identifying the member segments that have the highest retention risk. Once that is accomplished, you can determine what action to take.

• **Compare your association to other organizations.** Chapters of a national association often want to compare retention rates. After all, they all have the "same" type of member. But other factors, such as geography, also can serve as the basis for comparisons. For instance, the Washington, D.C., metropolitan area has a lot of churn (turnover in its population). Compared to many other geographic areas, it has a higher percentage of people moving in and out.

The major pitfall in comparing retention rates—whether with an association in the same field or in the same city—is that each organization has its own particular mix of members, programs, and resources. Special criteria may apply as well, such as mandatory membership in a national organization. These variances can make comparisons difficult and often not worth the effort.

Factors Affecting Retention

myth 5

There is one ideal retention rate.

reality

Retention is a complex process affected by various forces. It is unique to each association. The retention rate may vary over time, depending on what is happening in the association's and members' environments.

What is a good retention rate? There's no single quick answer to that question, which is not unlike answering "What does it cost to build a house?" Retention depends on a variety of factors, including:

• **The effects of economic and industrial change.** Changes in the economy and within an industry can have a tremendous effect on a membership organization. But associations often find that changes lag, sometimes from one to several years, before they affect retention. This lag is built into the system because most memberships expire yearly; when the time comes to renew, downsizing policies instituted during the previous 12 months may have taken effect. Conversely, some associations find that their membership retention is counter-cyclical—their rates go up when the economy slumps, and vice versa.

The plight of one national trade association demonstrates how quick and devastating an industry shift can be. In the late 1980s, this association had more than 200 members. Within 18 months its membership had dropped to below 50 because of merger-and-acquisition activities and purchases by international corporations. A major shift in leadership occurred as the mergers created five large organizations within the industry. The entire complexion of the industry changed almost overnight, and that kind of situation can't help but affect what an association is and does.

Technological development also can affect the retention rate. Today you won't hear of any National Association of Slide Rule Manufacturers; technology and the marketplace made the slide rule obsolete.

Sometimes opportunities and threats arrive as a package deal. When national, state, or local legislation threatens to affect an industry or profession, prospective members are often more interested in joining so the association can help protect their interests. Of course, the problem is retaining these members after the threat is eliminated. Waging a winning battle can be a very effective retention tool.

• **Who pays the dues.** Who pays for membership dues can affect retention rates, particularly for individual members. There appears to be a higher retention rate when the employer, rather than the individual, pays the dues. Retention rates are likely to suffer as more employers looking to cut costs pare back individual and organizational memberships.

• **Changes in demographics and lifestyles.** As Baby Boomers age or older members retire or die, younger members may not step in to replace them in equal numbers. Service organizations in particular have been hard-hit by women's increased participation in the workforce since the 1970s. Younger women, now working, have less time than their predecessors to volunteer their services and take an active role in these organizations.

The League of Women Voters dealt with the issue of less time by emphasizing in its promotional materials that members can support the league's efforts simply by joining and maintaining membership; they don't have to be active participants. Other organizations have formed separate "junior" chapters that revolve around the schedules and interests of younger working women.

In responding to demographic and lifestyle changes, associations are changing the way they do business. Instead of tours and shopping trips, spouse programs at annual conferences include seminars on topics such as stress management. Or the entire conference has been revamped because it can double as a family vacation. On the other hand, others are dropping spouse or children's events completely because they have found that more members travel alone to the conference.

Through member feedback, the Special Libraries Association discovered that its members had trouble finding the time for continuing education seminars. In addition, members attending its annual conference wanted to take advantage of airline fares that favor weekend stay-overs. The association addressed those needs simultaneously by offering educational seminars on the Saturday and Sunday preceding the conference. An extra benefit: The seminars provide new revenue for the association. The Special Libraries Association also offers professional and cultural field trips on the day after its conference concludes. These are popular with price-sensitive segments of the membership who use the conference as the core of their annual vacation.

By looking at the unique characteristics and demographics of your membership as part of an annual member needs assessment, you'll be in a good position to take advantage of the opportunities afforded by changing lifestyle patterns.

• **Actions of key influencers.** Key influencers, also known as market leaders, are the people and organizations that everyone else in the field knows of and often follows. Sometimes they're the first to adopt new products or pioneer new services and can bring additional credibility to an association.

While you should try to attract and retain key influencers, it's important not to become totally reliant on one or two—especially for supporting major activities such as annual conferences and trade shows. Doing so could make these events too dependent on the shifting winds of commerce and societal change. Should a significant change occur in a key influencer's business or career, the association could be hard-hit. Also, it's risky to give one or two members too much control over the entire association.

• **The competition.** When competition heats up between similar associations or between an association and a vendor, retention can be negatively affected. For example, one association's key benefit was its sponsorship of the industry's premier trade show. Unexpectedly, a Fortune 100 company (a member) decided to sponsor a competing show. As a result, the association's income and retention rate fell dramatically.

However, the fastest growing competitive factor to retention is not another organization but your members' limited time and money, both on the job and personally. They may not want to, or cannot, give up time to participate in the association.

• **Additional factors.** Other common trends affecting retention include a reduction in the number of associations to which people belong and shared memberships within an organization. (In the latter situation, one person rather than three may join an association and share the materials received with the other two people.) Also, some companies have reduced the number of institutional memberships they hold to cut costs.

Although a drop in retention may accompany a dues hike, if members feel that they are receiving value for their dues they will be less sensitive to a price increase. Associations reduce the risk of membership loss by careful planning in advance of the increase. This includes orchestrating presentations that explain the reasons for the increase, instituting a gradual rather than radical dues increase, and communicating a positive perception of membership value.

Based on a combination of the factors above plus others unique to your association and its members, you'll be able to determine the "right" retention rate. Just remember that what is a reasonable retention rate for Association X isn't likely to be the same for Association Y. Using attrition and retention rates properly can provide tangible measurements for the many intangibles associated with providing service to members. These rates can become rallying points and sources of pride for the staff and volunteers who have worked hard to keep your association vital.

Chapter 4

Customer Service = Member Satisfaction = Retention

Strategic retention, as discussed in Chapter 2, means delivering the goods to members, whether in the form of tangible products and services or intangible benefits. *How* you deliver those goods is what member or customer service is all about. And how well you satisfy members with both the goods and the delivery will have a direct bearing on whether they retain their membership.

Members as Customers

Your members are customers of the association purchasing membership as well as other products. However, unlike customers of a retail operation or a company, your members are also part owners of the establishment they're patronizing. Association members feel a loyalty that many for-profit organizations envy and hope to replicate through customer retention strategies such as frequent flyer or buyer clubs.

But just because they have a sense of belonging and ownership doesn't mean members will tolerate less than satisfactory products and service. In fact, they usually expect a high level of service from "their" association. After all, they're paying the bills. It's not unusual for staff to hear phrases such as, "I pay your salary," "I deserve better," and "I am your boss."

myth 6

High nondues revenues eliminate retention worries.

reality

Members form the primary customer base for most associations; to lose members is to lose customers. If all your members disappeared tomorrow, so would your market base for nondues revenues.

That's why it's crucial to identify members' expectations from the start; you can't satisfy needs you don't know about. As one association meeting planner said, "Nothing is so frustrating as to read an evaluation after a meeting about a problem I could have fixed if someone had mentioned it to me during the meeting." Research efforts can be formal, including focus groups and surveys, or based on information available through the association's historical files. Membership-based organizations don't always maximize their critical competitive advantage of definitively knowing their primary customers—their members.

Through your research you'll undoubtedly encounter the White Hat Syndrome—the idea that the association is viewed as the "good guys" who always play fair and maintain and demonstrate high standards of integrity. It's a double-edged sword. Members do a lot for their association, volunteering time and resources, as well as sharing their expertise, and they expect a lot in return. Many an association has learned hard lessons about violating the white-hat syndrome, usually via member complaints and even resignations.

A Money-Back Guarantee

Many associations report that offering a money-back guarantee has encouraged more members to try their products and services, whether it's attending the annual conference or buying a book. They also report that members rarely use the guarantee's refund option.

Considering a member's lifetime value, the refund is normally a small cost relative to the benefits, especially if it saves the membership. When a member does request a refund, it is usually someone with a specific complaint. Offering the refund can be the first step toward converting a dissatisfied member back to a satisfied one. But it is only a first step. You must also identify any underlying issues leading to the dissatisfaction.

Great Expectations

Identifying and meeting expectations would be relatively simple if your association operated in a vacuum, if no changes occurred throughout the industry or profession or the world at large. Like most people, your members expect consistency and predictability and they often base their expectations on past experience. Suppose your association always has had a continental breakfast at morning meetings; members expect a continental breakfast at the next morning meeting unless advised differently.

When you change what or how you deliver—which is bound to happen because change is inevitable—also plan how to change members' expectations. If, for example, you usually hold meetings on the third Thursday of the month and decide to switch to the second Monday, it's not enough to simply change the date in the normal meeting announcement. Instead, highlight the change with larger or bolder type or print the announcement on a different color of paper—whatever it takes to capture members' attention. Also helpful is explaining why you've made the change (for example, the meeting space is free of charge on Mondays). Otherwise, members will expect what they've gotten in the past.

Explanations are also in order if changes resulting from unforeseen circumstances may affect the association's response time (for example, most of the staff is out sick or attending the annual conference). An explanation, if communicated properly, helps to change members' expectations. Most members are reasonable and will accept the explanation, which can help decrease and possibly eliminate their dissatisfaction.

Before making a change, analyze whether it will make life easier for the members or for the staff—ideally it will do both. Cost is always a factor in the decision-making process, but sometimes the greatest cost is member dissatisfaction. A change that makes sense from a staff efficiency standpoint, for example, may create so much ill will among members that it backfires. This is more likely if members perceive the change as a reduction of services and underscores the importance of implementing change properly.

Put simply, it's not enough to do the right things. They also must be done right. Even "quality" training can be done poorly. So it's not only *what* you do but *how* you do it.

A research survey conducted by The Gallup Organization asked people to define "quality in service." Respondents identified three key ingredients: courtesy, attitude, and helpfulness of staff. Another survey, one conducted by the White House Office of Consumer Affairs, found that dissatisfied customers, on average, tell nine other people about their bad experience; satisfied customers tell five people. This study also found that every complaint an organization receives represents an average of 26 other dissatisfied

Techno-Talk

"I don't know who this new phone system was designed for, but it certainly does not make life easier for the member," someone remarked about an association's most recent foray into new technology—which, ironically, had been changed to improve member service.

Like any tool, technology handled poorly can be a disaster; handled well it can enhance retention. But first it must be the right technology for the members. Are they technologically phobic or literate? Do they see technology as a positive or as something to avoid? Is it important for their association to be on the cutting edge of technology?

In addition, what do they need? For instance, members who demand a very high level of personalized service may always want access to a "real" person when they call your association, even if they initially hear a voice-mail message. Some associations have managed members' expectations by phasing in voice mail gradually, first using an operator who offers the options of taking a message or forwarding the caller to voice mail and then dropping this interim step.

In the example above, the association's new phone system may have been the right technology but wasn't implemented properly. Smart association CEOs avoid problems like this by testing new technology systems on a pilot basis and debugging them before full implementation.

customers who don't bother to complain. That's not surprising. After all, think about how many times you've stopped dealing with a vendor without first indicating your dissatisfaction.

Within associations, which pride themselves on close relationships with members, these survey results are magnified. Little things—the way a phone is answered or a message left—can turn into large issues. For instance, one regional trade technology association conducted member focus groups and received positive feedback about its overall operations. But one criticism related to telephone procedures surfaced repeatedly. As one member explained, "I am asked to spell my name and the name of my company even if I am returning their call. What adds insult to injury is that since we have under 1,000 members, the association could put a device on the phone so the caller's name and any other information you want to add, such as the company, come up on the screen automatically. This is a technology association, and yet they are like the shoemaker's children who have no shoes." The association had no inkling that its common practice was generating such negative feelings. No one had ever mentioned it to the staff. But the situation, once identified, was easily rectified.

Some associations fare better with their members when it comes to satisfaction with big-ticket items, such as lobbying for an important piece of legislation or developing top-quality conferences and publications. Yet the small stuff, such as answering the phones, can also influence membership retention decisions.

The Royal Treatment

The Gallup research implies that people can become satisfied customers on the basis of how they're treated. Members who don't get what they want may still be satisfied if handled properly. By training staff and key volunteers in customer-service techniques, you increase the likelihood that members will walk away satisfied.

For example, the Disney properties, which are well-known for their excellent customer service, consider staff members who deal directly with visitors to be "on stage"; all other personnel have supporting roles and are considered "backstage." Disney had to reclassify at least one position when it found that visitors talked most frequently to its street cleaners. As a result, Disney began to provide the formerly backstage street cleaners with on-stage training in customer service and in how to answer the most frequently asked questions.

Who has the most contact with your association's members? Perhaps accounting (for billing problems), member records (for changes to name and contact information), or fulfillment (for purchasing problems)? Or might it be your receptionist who, even with voice mail, has the most initial contact with members? If you track incoming calls, you might be surprised to find out which staff members talk with members the most. That finding has prompted some associations to not only provide all staff with customer-service training but also to institute a service or information center.

You may also want to identify the complaints, problems, and compliments that surface in members' calls. Even after a problem has been solved, it is useful to see if patterns or trends emerge. By tracking and analyzing types of calls, you can take steps to reduce or even prevent future problems as well as expand areas that generate member satisfaction. However, depending solely on unsolicited comments may be misleading. For a more accurate view of whether the service you provide is truly effective, you'll need formal input from members via surveys or other research methods.

Management guru Tom Peters views complaints as useful pieces of market intelligence. "Listening to complaints must become everyone's business. With most competitors moving ever faster, the race will go to those who listen (and respond) most intently," he writes in *Thriving on Chaos: Handbook for a Management Revolution.*

At Your Service

The majority of calls coming in to the American Society for Quality Control (ASQC) are handled by a centralized service center. Its 40 employees take immediate action on members' inquiries and orders and also assist nonmembers in purchasing ASQC's quality-related products and services.

In addition to receiving special training, the service center staff are monitored for their courteous and professional service, knowledge of ASQC's products and services, and efficiency in responding to the 45,000 calls that pour in during an average month. Ranked in descending order, the most frequent types of calls involve information requests, orders for products or services, and status of order/inventory inquiries (billing, delivery, back orders, etc.). Any calls the service center can't handle (approximately 35 percent) are referred to the appropriate staff member.

According to ASQC's annual research, this one-stop shopping concept has exceeded all customer expectations.

It would be unrealistic to say that you can always satisfy every member of your association. Some people will be dissatisfied and complain no matter what you do. Unfortunately, these eternally dissatisfied members can take up a disproportionate amount of your time. The good news, however, is that most associations don't have large numbers of such members. If staff can solve the problem, or in some cases if they can't solve it but still are responsive, the "reasonable" dissatisfied customer or member will be satisfied and remain loyal to your organization.

In the Know

Imagine discovering that a staff member didn't know about a major membership retention effort underway at your association. When that happened at a regional individual membership association, the CEO lamented, "I learned about this shortcoming from a board member who had to inform

Keeping the Staff Satisfied

Given the key role that staff members play in delivering member services, it follows that they'll do a better job if satisfied themselves. As with members, satisfaction starts with expectations—in the form of clear-cut employee performance standards that appear in written job descriptions and operating procedures. Employees who meet or exceed those expectations should be rewarded accordingly.

Establishing standards for member contact can start with answering telephone calls, the lifeline to members. Examples include answering calls by the third ring, returning calls within 24 or 48 hours, and ensuring that the person who takes a call has responsibility for providing an answer either personally or indirectly (this helps to avoid telephone tag). As another example, staff might be instructed to pass along any unsolicited feedback from members to the person or department who delivered the service. Most staff members want to do a good job, and that calls for both positive feedback and constructive criticism.

To ensure they have the right tools for the job, staff require appropriate information and training. Just as you send employees to training sessions on the use of computer software or hardware, you should provide training in the "soft" skills relating to member and customer service. Typical training topics include dealing with difficult people, listening skills, and teamwork. Also helpful are guidelines for decision making, so staff know how empowered they are to address problems without fear of reprimand.

the staff person about the campaign. Imagine my embarrassment. Never again will that happen—I've added all staff to the member mailing list."

The membership director of a national professional association adds another wrinkle, saying, "If you go to different departments and ask the same question, you are likely to get different answers. We are losing members who feel we are not well-managed, since the left hand does not know what the right hand is doing!"

In both situations, information is at the heart of the matter. Members assume that staff and key volunteers know about the association and can provide consistent and accurate information. Both groups, therefore, should have a general understanding of the association's structure, operations, and basic products. Often associations accomplish this by providing an orientation session and manual to new staff members and new volunteers. Another idea is to ensure staff read your association's primary publications as well as mailings of general interest to all members.

Providing such information helps discourage the philosophy of "it's not my job" and encourages a greater interest in the association as a whole. Plus, the practice may lead to the cross-selling of existing products and the development of new products and services as people in different departments identify similar areas of interest and possible opportunities for collaboration.

> **❝We do a significant amount of research that tells us what the issues of satisfaction are and position our organization to have unfailingly good customer service. We want service to be a hallmark of our approach, and we know our members recognize us for that customer satisfaction.❞**
>
> —*Paul Borawski, executive director, American Society for Quality Control*

Are Members Always Right?

Given today's emphasis on service, staff members may sometimes feel that they're caught in the middle, trapped between an unreasonable member or request and the policies of the association. You want to provide good, consistent service to the members so you establish policies along those lines—then a member demands you break the policy in the name of service.

"Sometimes the officers are the worst in asking us to break the rules, just for them, as if no one else would find out. The last time I 'bent' policy for an officer, he bragged to the other members about his clout and then I got the other members complaining to me! Never again," says one association executive. Adds another, "When I nicely explain the policies, they say since it is *their* association, can't we make an exception?"

Such situations clearly pose a service dilemma. On one hand, it's easy to say "Break the policy." After all, doesn't the customer or member always come first? Isn't the customer or member always right? But if you bend or break the rules for one member, you're essentially setting a new standard. Or you're accused of playing favorites. In response, some associations now provide training to all staff and volunteers on how to handle a member who is dissatisfied or unreasonable. The goal is satisfied members—not necessarily members who always get what they want.

When staff is clear on what they're supposed to do to identify and meet members' expectations—and when they handle the small things properly—the result is an association with a powerful ability to serve and satisfy members. By focusing on member satisfaction:

• **Retaining members will be easier than recruiting replacements.** As previously noted, research into customer satisfaction indicates that it's 5 to 15 times harder to attract a new customer than to keep an existing one. (This factors in all the time spent on prospects that fail to materialize.)

Although not aimed specifically at associations, these findings certainly should be of concern. For associations with narrowly defined membership prospect pools, the numbers might be even higher. It makes sense that staff and volunteers can reduce their work by keeping the members and customers they already have.

• **Satisfied members will sell the association to prospects.** Satisfied members give your association an image of being a "can-do" organization, and they're more willing to recruit new members through both formal member-get-a-member campaigns and informal word-of-mouth advertising. One member of the National Cattlemen's Association even offers to front the dues for selected reluctant prospects. He tells them that if the association doesn't meet their needs, they don't have to pay him back. (He's been repaid by 100 percent of the members who took advantage of his offer.)

• **Life will be easier for staff members.** Imagine how much more productive staff could be if you eliminated 5, 10, or even 15 percent of member complaints. They'd have that much more time to spend on developing new programs and services. When members are satisfied, staff will find their work is easier and more pleasant.

• **You'll sell more goods and services.** Your association is a brand, and satisfied customers develop a brand loyalty. If members feel that your association has an excellent track record for products and services, they'll be more likely to buy additional offerings and to tell their colleagues about the good service they receive. One of those goods and services, of course, is membership.

Member/customer service is an all-staff function, not just the job of membership. It is a key tool for the association's goal of increasing membership retention. It is both the right and the smart thing to do to improve the lives of the members, the staff, and the CEO. It makes the association a healthier place to work and is truly a win-win situation for all.

Chapter 5

Packaging the Value

Whether your members are individuals or organizations, you provide value in both tangible and intangible ways. Your association's membership marketing piece, for example, probably lists highly tangible benefits such as publications and conferences. Those can be seen, held in the hand, or otherwise experienced physically. Yet many benefits are intangible, such as promoting ethical conduct, creating a positive perception of your industry or cause among consumers, and simply generating a good feeling of belonging and pride in your association and what it represents.

"Does your organization invest in improving things that do not result in increased loyalty or retention? Do you improve things that the organization thinks are important but overlook improvements that really matter to the customers?" asks Alexandra Lang in the ASAE *Membership Marketer*. Those questions underscore the relationship between value and retention. Simply put, members will want to retain membership in your organization if they believe it's valuable to them.

The relationship between value and retention is very simple: If there is value, members will want to retain their memberships. The hard part for CEOs and their

myth 8

The staff knows what our members want.

reality

A good staff certainly knows about members—but only from a staff perspective. The best way to obtain the member perspective is to ask members themselves. Investing in research provides you with the facts, which is always better than making an educated guess.

associations is in determining what is valuable to a member. The key to providing value is to identify and respond to the needs of the member in a way that the member perceives to be valuable (whether the member is an organization or an individual). Generally, the association provides value by developing products. If these products meet the members' perceived needs, then the products should positively affect the bottom line, which, for associations, is membership retention.

At one time, providing value meant making sure the right product at the right price got to the right customer. The idea of "right" was based on meeting the wants and needs of a customer. Although the importance of those concepts hasn't changed, members have. Today they expect not just service but *individualized* service to meet their expectations.

> **❝We will get into something if our members need it. If the market is taking care of it, we'll stay out.❞**
>
> —*Garis Distelhorst, CAE, executive director, National Association of College Stores*

In response, you must recognize members as individual customers of the association, identify their individual expectations as much as possible, and then exceed those expectations whenever possible. Because it's unlikely that you can exceed individual expectations all the time, the secret is to always meet expectations.

Seeing is Believing

"Perception is 100% of the game." This pearl of wisdom, usually attributed to Tom Peters, communicates a truth that must be relearned daily. All producers of goods and services, including membership organizations, are inherently egocentric. Their view is from the inside out, from the association looking toward its members. It's a conscious struggle to do the opposite, to see from the outside in or from the customer's perspective.

Perception of value has two major components: positioning in the mind and usefulness. The value of anything your association produces or does for its members resides in the mind of members. Outside the members' minds, the publications, conferences, seminars, or whatever, are just an assortment of items sitting in a valueless vacuum. But when a member has a specific want or need, then the corresponding object or activity has value.

Advertising experts Jack Trout and Al Ries address this concept in *Positioning: The Battle for Your Mind*. "Positioning is thinking in reverse," they write. "Instead of starting with yourself, you start with the mind of the prospect. Instead of asking what you are, you ask what position you already own in the mind of the prospect."

In the mind of a member, a product's position relates directly to its usefulness. And the usefulness of a product or service depends on how easily the customer or member can translate what is offered into what they want or need. This act of translation can be characterized by the question "So what?"—an excellent question about every product and service you provide, to be asked from the members' perspective. The answers may be surprising. You may find, for example, that even though your publication contains lots of information, your members are unable to translate most of it into something useful to their businesses or professions.

"Members are basically very self-centered," observes an association CEO. "Value is based on what they want at that particular time. If you're not offering that, you're in trouble."

The basic membership scenario plays out this way:

1. Potential member has a need.

2. Association addresses that need.

3. Potential member joins association, expecting it to fulfill the need.

4. Association fulfills the need.

5. Member renews because the need is fulfilled.

6. Association continues to fulfill the need.

7. Member continues to retain membership—until one day the member's need changes or the association stops fulfilling the need.

8. Member does not renew because the need was not fulfilled.

The one constant throughout the process is the member's need. Everything goes fine as long as the association understands and keeps in touch with members' current and future needs through research. As soon as a need changes, the relationship between the member and the association changes.

A Package Deal?

Some associations attempt to address members' needs by providing an entire package, or bundle, of products and services—whether or not the particular member needs them all. Typically, the benefits bundled with membership include a "free" subscription to the association's publication, a "free" membership directory, and legislative or promotional efforts undertaken on behalf of the entire association, industry, or profession. This practice can turn association products into the equivalent of junk mail, something people didn't request and don't want. Members then perceive the product to have no value to them and consider it a waste of their dues.

To deal with this classic problem of value, many associations have separated (or unbundled) the products offered as part of their paid membership. Some, especially those charging high annual dues, still offer the option of "free" publications and research reports as part of membership. But these associations usually ask members which publications they want to receive, thus eliminating the members' perception of "junk," of paying to receive something they don't value.

Other associations have gone a step farther. While members still automatically receive some benefits as part of paying dues, they have the option of purchasing other benefits separately. This cafeteria-type plan provides not only choice but also nondues revenue for the association. For some associations this is a minor part of their income, with the majority coming from dues. For a growing number of associations, however, nondues income has become the primary source of revenue.

Based on their perceptions, members pay for the products they value. Unbundling allows them to choose which association products they want and need and creates a perception of overall value that can have a positive influence on the retention decision. The practice also acknowledges that different segments of the membership value different benefits. Each member can tailor the package of membership benefits to fit his or her needs—an important aspect of individualized service.

As helpful as unbundling may be for members, it places an added burden on staff. When products are packaged together as automatic benefits of membership, your association has a built-in market. Whether or not a product interests members, they get it (and it's subsidized by their dues). When unbundled, however, each product or service must be marketed separately and stand on its own financially. In the open market, it becomes immediately evident which products are responsive to member needs.

Getting Picky

As unbundling increases and the number of nondues revenue offerings rises, you're apt to see *cherrypicking*. This refers to picking the best and leaving the rest. For associations this selective practice takes two forms.

The first is cherrypicking membership. These people join the association every few years, usually staying in for only one year at a time. Often they'll rejoin after a major revision of materials or the introduction of an expensive product that carries a significant discount for members. They repeatedly reap the rewards of being a "new" member by letting their membership lapse. In between, these on-again-off-again members cherrypick key products to receive the benefits of membership "on the cheap" without retaining their membership.

The second more widespread and growing form is when nonmembers cherrypick to buy key products in lieu of joining. Some of these nonmembers purchase many products a la carte—and their numbers appear to be growing. For example, they may want to attend only the annual trade show or subscribe to the leading research publication in the field.

Nonmembers often know about products, services, and meetings because their names remain on an association's mailing list indefinitely. Even prospects who have never been members are put on mailing lists as potential purchasers of products. If your association maintains a database with profiles of members and nonmember purchasers and their purchasing histories, an analysis will show if cherrypicking has become a critical issue and correlates with a declining retention rate. If so, you may want to restructure your membership offers or increase the differential between fees paid by members and nonmembers. Another alternative is to restrict certain products or benefits to members. By testing various packaging and pricing strategies, you can identify ways to discourage this potentially membership- and revenue-draining practice.

Golden Handcuffs

Most associations would like to have a golden handcuff—a benefit considered so valuable that a member would still belong even if the association terminated all other membership benefits. Such a benefit ensures a stable membership, essentially through a captive audience.

Timothy P. Watson, on the staff of a county medical society, jokingly envisioned the ultimate golden handcuff: "As a medical society, we need to develop the technology for eternal life. Members would be granted eternal life as long as they retained membership. We would no longer have a retention problem since if you dropped your membership, you would die."

Needless to say, not a real-world situation (although it would probably generate a 100-percent retention rate). In the real world, a golden handcuff can vary from an insurance program to a professional designation, from a premier publication to a well-regarded awards program. On the up side, a highly prized benefit supports membership retention (the handcuff) because members feel they can't survive without it (the gold). The downside is resentment toward the handcuffs, especially if members feel that an unresponsive monopoly is holding them captive.

Even with a golden handcuff or two, an association cannot assume that all its retention issues are resolved. For instance, some associations that had one-of-a-kind products found that the market changed or became so attractive that competitive products appeared. This resulted in a quick loss of market share, loss of income and—if the product was the primary reason for joining—loss of membership.

For the Grand Rapids Home Builders Association, member involvement is the golden handcuff that contributes to the association's high retention rate. The 1,100-member association has 72 committees, most of which meet monthly and have formal agendas, minutes, and a staff liaison. The committees, on which a majority of members serve, have taken on many community projects and are very visible in the Grand Rapids area.

From a retention perspective, the ultimate golden handcuff is the overall package of products and services. If you focus on being indispensable to members and design an array of products to meet members' changing needs, you'll give members an excellent reason for renewing.

Making Adjustments

The primary benefit of membership in one specialized legal association was its monthly publication, the cost of which was included in the membership dues. In attempting to cover the most recent developments in pertinent legislation—an activity that harkened back to its early years—the association began to miss deadlines and distribute the journal behind schedule.

Through focus groups, the association discovered that the legislative information it was trying so hard to include was actually too little and too late for members to use. Instead, most members subscribed to a weekly trade publication that covered legislative issues in a more timely and in-depth manner than the association's monthly journal. Members, however, remained pleased with the journal's in-depth specialized articles.

When the staff compared the weekly trade publication's subscriber list to the association's membership list, they found more than 95-percent overlap. Most of the nonsubscriber members were retired or non-practicing members. After validating the research, the association dropped the legislative coverage from its monthly journal to concentrate on in-depth articles. But first, staff informed the membership of the decision and arranged for a special discount offer to the weekly publication for non-subscribing members.

Although the association missed a market opportunity for a weekly publication, it restructured its monthly publication in response to members' needs. The journal went from being a source of dissatisfaction to a benefit that generated satisfaction.

Developing Products to Meet Member Needs

Products of associations reflect their different members and unique needs. The following are a few examples of some popular categories of association products.

1. Information-based products. Because of the relationship they've established with members, associations are in an ideal position to collect information on an industry, profession, cause, donor, or customer group—data that members may be reluctant to give to an outside third-party vendor. Some of these information-based products complement existing commercial or governmental products, while others refine and add value to existing statistics such as census data. The American Ceramic Society offers access to more than 150,000 abstracts via print, on-line, and CD-ROM products; the Michigan Manufacturers Association sponsors a human resource information line.

Some association information databases are available through on-line services such as Dialogue. Their usage generates a revenue stream for the association as well as publicity and recognition for the association and its members. It also means members can access the information they need when they need it, regardless of time zones, association operating hours, and staffing patterns. For instance, members of the American Chamber of Commerce Executives can tap into ChamberNet at any hour for access to association and local government databases, electronic mail, bulletin boards, U.S. Congress listings, and commercial information services such as Newsgrid and the Official Airlines Guide.

An association library or information center can be an important benefit because it offers information kits and bibliographies on hot topics of interest to members, free or for a fee. Some associations have a unique collection of materials that members can use on site or access via phone, fax, or computer. Those materials may include samples of products and internal research studies, which are valuable to both staff and members who hope to avoid reinventing the wheel. Association libraries often undertake small research projects for members without charge; in other cases, they do customized research projects on a fee basis. A focus group participant from the American Society of Corporate Secretaries summed it up when he said, "Getting the right answer quickly more than paid for my dues."

2. Products developed by chapters. The New York City chapter of the American Marketing Association publishes a reference book that lists research firms. Because the book has a national audience, the New York City chapter has a royalty agreement with other chapters that sell copies of it. The book not only creates a large revenue stream for the New York City chapter but also gives it nationwide recognition.

National associations often find it useful to keep tabs on the products developed at regional and local levels for possible national distribution. Likewise, local, state, and regional associations sometimes find profit in modifying or selling products produced by sister organizations.

3. Catalogs. Like many organizations, the Optical Society of America uses its catalog to sell existing products, primarily technical books and electronic products. But it also uses the catalog to recruit authors and editors in areas in which the society wants to expand. One edition requested "educational material that will aid in the teaching of optics on the high school or college level" and noted the society's willingness to work with other publishers or sister societies to produce or market books or proceedings.

Unlike commercial catalogs, association catalogs often spell out the group's mission and describe membership opportunities. When members of the American Bankers Association receive a catalog, they see lists of publications as well as descriptions of ABA educational conferences and related products. ABA's catalog also includes photographs and testimonials of members.

4. Consortiums and partnerships. Associations have a long history of partnerships with vendors to offer member benefits such as insurance programs and car rentals (often called affinity programs). More recently they have worked out partnerships with other associations, governmental agencies, and private-sector organizations. As an example, the American Association of Retired Persons publishes a pamphlet entitled "Healthy Questions" in cooperation with the Federal Trade Commission. It tells members and non-members alike how to talk to and select physicians, pharmacists, dentists, and vision care specialists.

By forming partnerships, your association can maximize its ability to achieve its mission and meet the needs of members. It allows you to offer additional services or products that you couldn't afford on your own.

5. Products for members' customers. A number of associations publish materials for members to distribute or sell to their clients. These range from informational newsletters to educational brochures and often include space for members to print their own name, such as those done by the American Academy of Family Physicians. The American Library Association, for example, produces posters, T-shirts, buttons, and other items that public libraries sell to promote reading, as well as to raise funds.

Creating value for members is an unending process, the ultimate success of which is measured by membership retention. As your members' needs change, so must your products. That evolution has led several chapters of the American Institute of Architects to operate stores that sell books, gifts, and design-oriented merchandise to the general public. The American Dental Association translated changing member needs into a home mortgage program, while the National Speakers Association started offering audiocassettes to members as well as a print publication (after all, its members make their living by speaking). And when downsizing left some of its members without a full-time personnel department, the Pittsburgh High Technology Council began offering contract human resource services.

Another area of growth appears to be producing materials about an industry, profession, or cause geared to consumers—especially children. For example, the American Society of Mechanical Engineers produces a series of "Engineering is for Everyone" videotapes for kindergarten through Grade 6, plus the "Mothers of Invention" videotape for junior high audiences.

Whatever form they take, the best products are the ones that members value and view as an incentive to retain their membership.

Building Brand Equity

The corporate world considers a brand name an important and valuable asset because, over time, it becomes instantly recognizable to customers. Companies such as American Express and FedEx have built their business by equating their names with high standards for quality and service. It's not unusual for companies to bypass a new business opportunity if it doesn't fit with their corporate image or a brand's primary market. A good example is Disney, a brand synonymous with wholesome family fun; when the company decided to move into movies for adults, it created new divisions and brand names rather than risk confusing customers and losing brand equity. In other cases, companies delay the introduction of products until modifications can be made so nothing diminishes their brand name's reputation for quality.

Although the term is rarely used in the association industry, the concept of brand equity certainly applies. In fact, associations may have the edge when it comes to brand loyalty. Some CEOs believe that given the choice of an equivalent product offered by both a vendor and their membership organization, members will choose the latter.

But there's a price for building brand equity—you must continually meet the expectations of high quality and service. Every time you develop or re-evaluate a product, you must ensure it does not diminish the image you've developed through your other products. Members base much of their retention decision on perceived value. Having a reputation for quality goes a long way toward making that perception a positive one.

Rewriting the Book on Service

The primary product distributed by members of the National Association of College Stores (NACS) is textbooks. Still, member stores sell other books, but sometimes not in enough numbers to fulfill the restrictive sales policies of some book publishers. In stepped the association as an intermediary buyer, and its book buying service has grown into a multimillion-dollar business subsidiary over the last 32 years. NACS also developed a national program that saves many members up to 53 percent on their freight costs. In many cases, members' savings from the freight program exceed the "service fee" (NACS' term for membership dues).

NACS is also partnering with the Association of Research Libraries on the Electronic Reserve Room Project—a partnership that will improve the efficiency of copyright permissions for both university bookstores and libraries. NACS is also exploring the possibilities of other services that would help their members do business in a changing publishing environment.

Association Products and Services

Although by no means exhaustive, here's a list of products and services various associations offer to members and, in some instances, to nonmembers. Some are also sources of nondues revenue.

I.   Membership
   A. Member services
   B. Membership directory
      1. Advertising
      2. Sales to nonmembers
   C. Mailing lists
   D. Services and products relating to chapters or multi-level associations
   E. Special interest groups
   F. Vendor memberships

II. Meetings and conventions
   A. Meeting/conference program
   B. Exhibit/trade show
   C. Sponsorship of special events
   D. Advertising on-site program
   E. Special events for spouses and children
   F. Special seminars before/during/after meeting
   G. Promotional events for individual association products
   H. Sales of meeting cassettes/transcripts/photographs
   I. Fundraisers

III. Government affairs
   A. Legislative alerts and updates
   B. Analysis of proposed and final regulations
   C. Lobbying
   D. Meetings with legislators

IV. Publications and information services
   A. Books (including association manuals and workbooks and nonassociation publications)
   B. Periodicals/newsletters

continued on next pg.

C. Buyers guides and card packs
D. Reports
   1. Industry compilations and statistical reports
   2. Market or industry analyses
E. Directories
F. Information and research services
   1. Information center/library
   2. Topical bibliographies and information kits
   3. Access to databases
      a. Association-sponsored
      b. Resale of commercial services
   4. Customized research
   5. Member-sponsored surveys of their clients
   6. Research project underwritten by a specific group of members
   7. Public relations materials for members' use
   8. Teaching materials
G. Networking and communication services
   1. Peer directories
   2. On-line network
   3. Broadcast fax
   4. Fax on demand
   5. Videoconferencing
   6. Peer group meetings
H. Catalog
I. Nonprint materials (association or nonassociation products)
   1. Audiotapes
   2. Videotapes
   3. Computer related
      a. Hardware or software
      b. Evaluation of software or hardware

V. Education
A. Seminars, workshops, multi-day institutes
   1. By types of training

continued on next pg.

          a. Continuing professional education
          b. Management training
          c. Employee training programs for members
      2. By delivery media
          a. Live speakers
          b. Teleconferencing (audio or video)
          c. Cable
          d. Self-study programs
             1) Print
             2) Electronic

B. Certification, accreditation, competency-testing

C. Educational tours
   1. New markets
   2. New technology
   3. Prototype or excellent models

D. Other educational opportunities
   1. Mentoring programs
   2. Internships
   3. Apprenticeships
   4. Programs cosponsored with educational institutions
   5. Joint sponsorships (with affiliates/chapters)

E. Industry or profession standards/guidelines

F. Awards programs

VI. Individualized services

A. Placement/referral/executive search

B. Consulting/evaluation

C. Product testing or review

D. Arbitration

E. Association management

F. Other contract services

VII. Group purchasing programs

A. One-time purchases (equipment)

B. Ongoing purchases (affinity programs)

VIII. Association foundation or for-profit subsidiary

continued on next pg.

IX. Materials for members' use with their customers
   A. Informational brochures
   B. Newsletters, magazines
   C. Promotional materials

X. Miscellaneous
   A. Partnership programs with other associations, government, or corporate entities
   B. Grant programs from public and private sources
   C. Sponsorships
   D. Social action and philanthropic programs
   E. Rental of association property or facilities
   F. Credit union
   G. Store
      1. Sale of association-developed products
      2. Resale of non-association items
   H. Novelty items carrying association's logo
   I. Financial products, including mortgages

Chapter 6

Research for Retention

"We [association executives] often take our members for granted. We focus primarily on how to get more money out of them or why they leave. Two years ago I realized *we paid more attention and did more research with those that left than those that stayed.* That suddenly seemed incredibly stupid. We started doing more research with our existing members to find out why they stay, what they like, and what they need so we can know how to keep them—the members we already have."

—CEO Focus Group Participant

What do current members expect? What do they need? What products do they buy? How long have they belonged to the association? Only by researching questions like these can you truly provide the value that leads members to renew. Yet a surprising number of organizations devote more attention and money to researching why members leave.

Retention research falls into two categories: analyzing existing data and files (both from your association and external sources) and obtaining new information from primary research. Other books can tell you how to conduct both types of research effectively. Our objective is to look at how you can use that research to improve your association's retention process.

Start With What You Have

Business Week has noted that "A growing number of marketers are investing millions of dollars to build databases that enable them to figure out who their customers are and what it takes to secure their loyalty." Associations definitely have an advantage in this area: You already know who your members are. But you must find out what it takes to keep members loyal.

A good place to start is your membership files. Even if they're not organized into sophisticated databases, most provide a gold mine of information. Many associations are able to extract such information as:

- The average length of membership. This will help you determine life-time income and value (See Chapter 2).

- What types of members are more likely to purchase which seminars, books, or other specific products and services.

- Which and how many are "checkbook members"—whose only inter-action with the association is to send in an annual dues check.

- What percentage of total membership represents first-year members. Some associations that have a large percentage of new members report they need to rerun courses more frequently or take other actions targeted at this group, such as publishing a newsletter or holding orientation sessions just for them.

It's easier than ever to gather this type of information, especially if you begin as soon as a member joins. As Don Peppers and Martha Rogers explain in their book, *The One-to-One Future: Building Relationships One Customer at a Time,* "For what the marketer of 1950 would have spent to track all the information available about one customer, the marketer of [today] can track 4 million customers. The marketers who get the earliest start in exploiting this amazing asset will have a competitive edge for the lifetime of each customer they win at the starting gate."

Therefore, many associations find it helpful to get off to a fast start by building a prospect profile from the time of the first inquiry for information, purchase of any product or service, or request for a membership application. Ensure your database can accommodate information on *all* purchases, activities, and interactions by or with the member over time, in addition to personal information. You'll then have a tangible record of how the association has been of value to the member, as well as a database that can be a valuable research tool.

Right on Target

You can use these detailed records for targeted or database marketing, a process that analyzes usage data and then sends targeted communications (mailings, fax, e-mail, phone) to those who are the most likely purchasers. Targeted mailings to likely prospects based on a database analysis are more cost-effective than repeatedly mailing to unlikely purchasers. For example, a member who has attended several seminars per year for the last 15 years is more likely to attend future seminars than someone who joined at the same time but has never attended a seminar.

To cite Peppers and Rogers again, "Instead of trying to sell products to anyone who will buy them, with an emphasis on acquiring new customers, the 1:1 marketer tries to make sure that his company gets as great a share of each customer's business as possible." Particularly as some associations find their prospect membership pool shrinking (due to mergers, consolidations, and changes), this becomes a survival strategy.

Database marketing is heavily used in the private sector and is a growing trend in associations. The more you track—whether by type of product or topic of interest—the more sophisticated your analysis can become. You may, for example, identify which members are interested in regulations and legal matters based on their past purchases. Further tracking and analysis will reveal which members in this group prefer publications versus seminars.

A member's profile should also include unsolicited feedback, often in the form of telephone calls. Organized either by subject area or type of feedback, these comments may vary from complaints about a particular seminar to compliments on the association's new logo to questions about the new telephone system. One word of caution: While you should collect this feedback in order to identify areas requiring further analysis, don't rely on the feedback itself as valid research. Generally, self-selected respondents are not representative of the whole membership.

❝You need to know your members, their characteristics, demographics, culture, what makes them tick. Why are they members of the association? What are their functions? Then tailor programs and services to meet their needs.❞

—*Mary Jane Kolar, CAE, executive director, American Association of Family and Consumer Sciences*

Even when members do not renew, maintain historical files on them. An analysis of these files provides a comparison of who stays and who leaves, identifies what categories of members are most at risk of leaving (and perhaps should receive extra attention), and documents how products and services for certain segments may correlate with retention. You'll also have the information necessary to identify what non-renewers have in common with one another as well as what renewers have in common—and how the two groups differ.

Associations not only need to manage the process of collecting membership data; they also need to actively manage the process of sharing that information. For instance, if the publishing department has a list of people who have purchased books on marketing issues, it should share the list with the department creating a conference on the same topic. As logical as this sharing sounds, it can fall through the cracks if an association does not have a systematic procedure, such as accessing a centralized customer file, distributing files via an internal network, or designating contact people for various topics.

In addition to examining your own files, look to secondary research—data available from other sources such as the government, academia, and commercial research organizations. For instance, many organizations doing consumer research use the U.S. Bureau of the Census as a key source of secondary data. Public and special libraries abound with collections of industrial, professional, commercial, and governmental data and research. Locating secondary research can often reduce or even eliminate the need to conduct original research. The money and time you save can then be devoted to other retention-related activities.

Original Research

Once you have collected and analyzed existing data, you can conduct original research to fill in any gaps and to learn more about a particular membership area or issue confronting your members. Here are some of the questions you should answer:

• **Why do members join? Why do members retain their memberships?** The answers to these two questions may differ even for the same member. Another consideration: A member's answer about retaining membership may change over time. For instance, products important to new members, such as basic introductory courses, may lose their appeal when members are further along in their careers or when a company is at a different stage in its life cycle. Still, recurring patterns often emerge within segments or even the entire membership.

• **How can we be more responsive to member needs?** Ask your members to suggest new products as well as modifications to current products or to administrative procedures. It's not uncommon for research to prompt major changes in or outright elimination of an association's products. One CEO from a large national trade association puts it this way: "We used to just think up a new product at a staff meeting and run with it. Twenty years ago, that worked. Now our mistakes have gotten too expensive—in terms of lost dollars, time, and members. On the basis of lifetime value, I can justify research on a new product if it will reduce my mistakes. Sometimes it is as useful to learn what not to do, as what to do."

It also helps to do research with product non-users (including checkbook members) to see if you can identify barriers to purchasing a particular product and figure out if there is a way to overcome them. For example, one chapter of a national association discovered through research that many of its members, mostly entrepreneurs, didn't attend monthly meetings because they found it too difficult to get away from their businesses during the week. By moving its meetings to Saturday mornings, the chapter doubled attendance within three months.

• **How can we serve special segments more effectively?** Research will yield information specific to a membership group such as new members, vendors (often called associate members), international members, checkbook members, chapter members, or those from a subset of an industry or profession. Be sure you take full advantage of the knowledge and expertise of chapter officers if your association has international, national, regional, state, or local affiliates. The feedback from chapter officers can be crucial to clarifying and defining roles and can help identify how to increase cooperation and effectiveness to jointly retain members.

• **How are environmental changes affecting members?** Many associations report that their members place a high value on staying up-to-date on new trends and developments within their industry or profession. To meet that need, associations must keep on top of what's currently happening and what's projected for the future.

One good way to do that is by conducting extensive studies of the industry or profession and making the results available as a membership benefit or as a product that members can purchase. Another approach, taken by the

Bringing the Future Into Focus

The American Society of Corporate Secretaries (ASCS) commissioned six focus groups to determine how members perceived benefits, programs, and services and to gain information for future planning. Through the focus groups, different membership segments commented on enhancing, modifying, or discontinuing certain services; their perceptions of the association's name; and the value of the society's surveys, research services, educational programs, conferences, publications, and chapters.

The focus groups contributed significantly toward formulating short- and long-term strategies, and within a year ASCS had validated, tested, and implemented many of their members' ideas. Examples include:

• **Educational programs.** The focus groups indicated that the society's nuts-and-bolts course, "Essentials of the Corporate Secretarial Function," was a key benefit of membership and recommended offering an abbreviated version in conjunction with the national conference. The following year the society did just that. The seminar was not only oversubscribed but also generated high ratings as a pre-conference event.

The focus groups also suggested adapting the course to corporate secretaries of nonprofit organizations. After several seminars directed toward this market proved successful, ASCS formed a committee that specifically focuses on how the society could better meet the needs of this new membership segment.

• **Research services.** Compared to long-time members, newer members were generally unaware of research services available from the national office. Both groups indicated a willingness to pay for online services. Other ideas included converting selected publications, such as survey information, into a database.

• **Publications.** The focus groups suggested that ASCS prepare information kits on hot topics, supplement its newsletter with one-page bulletins on time-sensitive topics, and return to covering

continued on next pg.

chapter programs in the newsletter. As a result, the society developed a "newsgram" to highlight activities and projects undertaken by its 25 chapters. ASCS also began to study the feasibility of publishing a journal.

- **Networking.** Members participating in the focus groups asked for clarification of the services available and for more coordination of chapters at the national level. In response ASCS established a chapter liaison program, linking each chapter with one of six staff members. The chapter representative's job is to communicate with the chapter each month to gather ideas, learn about issues or concerns at the chapter level, and assist with membership campaigns and leadership development. Each representative attends at least one chapter meeting or regional conference to meet members and learn firsthand about their activities.

Optical Society of America, involves convening an expert panel of members to identify relevant emerging trends. The society used the findings to plan for state-of-the-art programs and publications.

- **How satisfied are our customers?** Customer satisfaction research typically concentrates on which products and services members value the most and what they think about the service the association provides. If structured appropriately, such surveys will yield data that can be analyzed by various membership segments or customer categories; you may detect patterns within one segment that don't apply to the others or to membership overall. Once you've established a baseline, you'll need to conduct research regularly to make ongoing comparisons.

You can use research to answer many other questions that relate to strategic retention. One association, for example, identified significant problems with its proposed public service announcements and was able to make corrections before televising them, thus avoiding potential embarrassment for members. The National Association of Life Underwriters has used focus groups to test and improve print materials, packets, and kits designed for prospects and new members. Other associations have used research to test the possible effects of changing their name or increasing their dues.

The Drop Zone

What's behind the decision not to renew an association membership? Based on the research conducted for this book, the following reasons emerged most frequently:

• Too expensive (not enough value).

• Not enough time to use membership.

• Dropping some of our memberships.

• Involved with another association that better fits my/our needs.

• Has nothing I (our organization) can use.

• Products don't fit our needs (too elementary, advanced, general, specific).

• No longer need membership because we are using a product from another source.

• It's a clique and I/we felt like an outsider.

• Bankruptcy or mergers, loss of employment, death.

• Changed profession/job/location/interest.

• Only heard from the association when you wanted our money.

• Member no longer meets membership requirements (including required continuing education).

• Employer no longer pays for it.

• Thought I/we had renewed.

• Never got an invoice.

Getting Answers Coming and Going

At a minimum, your retention process should include original research in two areas: Why members leave and what prompts prospects to become members.

Exit surveys, typically done through print questionnaires or one-on-one telephone interviews, may identify issues that you can address in order to reduce future losses. Sometimes non-renewing members who are contacted will reinstate their membership.

The exit interview is effective for identifying the straightforward reasons for membership loss, such as moving out of the area or changing jobs. Or, particularly with large or bureaucratic organizations, you may find out that members assumed their membership dues had already been paid. In the hands of a good interviewer, an exit interview can also zero in on more subjective reasons for not renewing, such as dissatisfaction with association benefits, a personality conflict with a volunteer or staff member, or the belief that a rival association better serves the member's needs.

However, not all non-renewing members may be so straightforward and specific. "I just don't feel like I'm getting enough out of the membership" and "The dues are too high" are common refrains. The meaning is the same: They perceive that they're not getting enough value for their money. Others may not want to give the real reason. As one association executive recalls, "My favorite story is the member who, when asked why he did not renew, told me that he had never received a dues invoice. We had sent him six, all to the correct address—I checked."

At the other end of the spectrum from exit interviews is determining the *closing, or conversion, rate*—how many of the prospects who request membership information actually join your association. People who initiate the request for membership information represent your most likely prospects. (Remember, retention begins with the first contact.) Anything you uncover in the course of researching prospects might apply to your members as well.

One association found that it had only a 30-percent closing rate. In other words, seven out of every 10 people who had expressed some interest in joining never did. Through research, the association identified several barriers to joining, including its complicated application form and complex dues structure. In addition to simplifying the application, the association improved its closing rate by encouraging applicants to call a staff member for assistance in calculating dues.

For another association, research confirmed that a delay in responding to inquiries led prospects to lose interest entirely or to become aggravated. Once the group improved the situation by assembling prospect kits in advance and using handwritten labels, it saw its closing rate increase dramatically. Other associations have found that a phone call to prospects from a volunteer or staff member within two or three weeks after the inquiry can improve the closing rate—as well as provide invaluable feedback from the prospects.

For instance, in the course of conversation, a prospect may say, "Your association seems to cater to large organizations." If that isn't your intention, you'll need to analyze the perception and address it, perhaps through something as simple as a change in the materials sent to prospects or a cover letter added from a member who falls into their category. Comments such as "I got information from both your association and your competitor and decided to join the other one" should lead you to compare your benefits package with the competition. Some associations have found that their benefits are better—but their competitors' benefits are better presented. That situation can be easily corrected.

A Good Investment

As helpful as exit surveys and new-member conversion research are, the most productive research addresses the needs and satisfaction issues of *current* members. Researching only those who leave is the equivalent of shutting the barn door after the horse has left. The earlier you take action, the more likely members will be to keep their membership. The decision to stay is often made well before the renewal invoice arrives.

Retention research is an investment in the future of your organization. By focusing on lifetime value, you can establish the value of each member—both economic and non-economic—to the association and underscore the importance of learning what members want. Done properly, research pays your association back by helping you retain more members for a longer time.

Hiring an Outside Research Firm

American Marketing Association's *State-of-the-Art Marketing Research* offers these suggestions for hiring a research firm:

- Identify two or three likely research firms. Casting your net too broadly wastes everyone's time.

- Make your first contact by letter, clearly stating the problem to be researched. Be sure to include an annual report and other helpful information about your organization.

- Get references and follow up on them.

- Interview your final selection of research firms to find out more about their research approach.

- Discuss the working relationship with prospective research firms. How often should progress reports be made and in what form (telephone, written correspondence, e-mail)? Will there be travel requirements? How long will the research take? What other resource requirements need to be discussed?

- Request a written proposal that clearly delineates price, schedule, and deliverables.

- Be sure to inform each prospective research firm that other firms are being considered.

- For large, extended studies, make provisions for mutually agreeable contract modifications.

- Identify primary contacts between client and researcher.

- Avoid rushing to an agreement. Further discussion could possibly change your association's research needs.

Chapter 7

Communicating With Your Members

I n researching this book, we asked 50 CEOs to describe their associations' retention efforts. One fundamental component of all answers was communication. Here's a sampling of what they said:

- "Retention is an entire association commitment [where] volunteers and staff...constantly inform the members of how [we] are working for them."

- "Reinforcing benefits via publications and meetings."

In the words of another CEO, all these answers point to the need for "Communications, communications!" Many members think of your association as being in the information business and, as a result, expect to receive informative communications. Those may take the form of newsletters telling members what you've done for them or telephone calls from the CEO or association staff to see how business is going for members. Whatever their format, these communications have a significant influence on the members' retention decision.

In the world of technical communications, primarily radio, people say, "I read you 5-by-5." Originally this phrase referred to the technical fidelity of a radio signal. Over time it has come to mean, "I read you loud and clear," a shorthand way of indicating that a communication link has been clearly established.

A 5-by-5 analogy appears in association communications, particularly when it comes to retention. The first set of five items relates to the elements of effective communications (how you're getting out your message). The second set of five items focuses on communications objectives (what you want the message to accomplish). As these 10 elements integrate and overlap, they support and advance your association's retention strategy. When members read you 5-by-5—loud and clear—they'll understand why it's important for them to remain in the association.

Characteristics of Communication

In *The National-Chapter Partnership: A Guide for the Chapter Relations Professional*, Patricia Newton, CAE, and Ginny Thiersch describe the five characteristics of effective communications. These characteristics, outlined below, apply to every aspect of your efforts and have major implications for retention:

1. Timeliness. In the association world of programs, seminars, and conferences, few crimes are greater than for members and other potential attendees to receive the promotional material after the event has occurred.

2. Appropriate frequency. How often do members hear from your association—once a month via an impersonal journal and in the three months leading up to their renewal date? Or, maybe they receive their journal on the same day as a convention promotion or a publications catalog—which may also be the same day a letter about insurance programs arrives?

It's doubtful that the member realizes multiple pieces of mail are from different departments. Rather, he or she perceives you're wasting dues dollars by sending several different items in several different envelopes all on the same day. These small annoyances can add up and sway the renewal decision; most important, they're avoidable through use of a master calendar of member communications or some other form of a coordinated mailing effort.

3. Appropriate format. Given the rapid development of electronic forms of communication, this is one area that is getting a lot of attention from many associations. Your members may feel most comfortable with traditional formats such as direct mail and print publications. However, a growing number of associations are using fax-on-demand, broadcast fax, e-mail, electronic bulletin boards, online newsletters, and other forms of communication. Decisions about what to use are complex. Major factors include the level of comfort your members have with technology and their hardware capabilities.

The CEO of a large medical association observes, "The members who use [our e-mail system] love it, but it is used by less than 1 percent of our membership. Our members are older and technology shy. As we recruit more young professional members, we expect the technology phobia of our membership will diminish." A vendor covers 100 percent of the system's costs, making it free to members of the association. Other organizations without such generous benefactors might consider an affinity program with a commercial online service or teaming up with other associations to offer a similar service.

4. Right audience. With this characteristic, associations really have the upper hand. By paying dues, members have self-selected themselves to be on your mailing list and to receive your communications. In contrast, commercial vendors must first identify their market and then persuade those people to open their mailings. That said, you can abuse the advantage through overmailing or sending out items or communications that members perceive as junk—as having no value. Make sure that you don't take your valuable audience for granted.

5. Proper implementation. You may have an informative newsletter available on an electronic service, but it loses value if members have difficulty accessing it. In other words, your communications can exhibit all of the four characteristics above and still not be effective because they aren't implemented properly.

Members judge their association's performance on the basis of what's visible, which is often the small stuff. If their association has trouble getting out mailings on time or can't spell names correctly, members will soon lose confidence in what they can't see, such as your ability to coordinate complex negotiations or represent their interests in the political arena.

Reasons to Communicate

What you'd like to accomplish through your communications is as important as how you approach them. There are five primary reasons for communicating with members; some occur individually or informally, some in combination or formally:

1. Identify members' needs. Every time you ask your members what they want and need, you're obtaining valuable feedback and research results. Formats vary tremendously and range from a few questions asked in a monthly newsletter, fax poll, or postcard survey to a full-blown focus group discussion, in-depth telephone survey, or multi-page print survey.

Associations often do this with a specific program objective in mind, such as determining the editorial direction of a key publication, deciding whether to change the format of the annual convention, or selecting legislative issues for your lobbyists to focus on. Perhaps some of the most critical issues are those concerned with triggering events—those points in time that the association can identify as key encounters with members.

For instance, receiving a membership application and dues check may trigger the association to make a welcoming phone call or send out a new member kit. Similarly, failure to renew may trigger an action such as a phone call or exit survey. Another key triggering event is when the new member signs up for his or her first meeting or session. For individual membership organizations, changes in job status may trigger members to re-evaluate whether they still have time to belong; assignment of a new key contact may trigger a trade association handling that replacement as a "new" member.

April 15 is a trigger event in the accounting world; no accounting association would hold a seminar the first week in April and expect people to come. Similarly, a number of associations have revised their schedule of surveys or seminars after researching members' lighter and heavier periods of activity. This kind of analysis and planning can have direct bottom-line implications. The better an organization can identify triggering events, the better it can prepare itself to respond to membership needs.

2. Contact members. Associations are primarily networks of individuals and institutions that feel a need to affiliate with others having similar interests and concerns. Consequently, your members often want, need, and, to some extent, demand contact. And by staying in close contact, your association demonstrates that it cares about its members.

Consider the experience of the Footwear Industries of America, which discovered that its members felt distanced being contacted only by mail. In response, the organization initiated a series of staff visits to individual member companies; according to Daniyel F. Steinberg's article in *Association Management*, relationships with members improved dramatically.

Contact covers a wide range of activities, from the very personal (face-to-face meetings) to the relatively impersonal (articles in publications).

3. Inform members of products, events, and issues. Perhaps the most prevalent objective in membership organizations is met through virtually every communication with members, from a calendar of upcoming events to a formal educational seminar, from a one-page fact sheet to a multi-day annual conference. In fact, the need for information is often a primary reason to join an association.

The Grand Rapids Home Builders Association dramatically emphasizes this need in its efforts to retain members. Members who don't renew receive a newsletter wrapper without a newsletter inside; it contains nothing other than a note saying, "We are sorry you didn't get this information." Other associations have used versions of this approach to underscore the void of information that results when members don't renew.

In researching this book, we asked experienced CEOs what advice they'd give to new CEOs regarding retention. The most common answer was, "Tell members what you're doing for them." In other words, don't assume that members see your association's accomplishments and give credit where it's due; be sure to tell them what you've accomplished.

4. Respond to members' needs. Membership organizations typically respond to members' needs quite well, as Peter Drucker once pointed out in a *Harvard Business Review* article. He instructed for-profit businesses that had lost contact with their customers in favor of short-term bottom lines to learn some lessons from non-profit organizations that, by virtue of their being membership organizations, need to stay close to their "customers." "Nonprofits also start with the environment, the community, the 'customers' to be; they do not, as American businesses tend to do, start with the inside, that is, with the organization or with financial returns," Drucker observed.

Responding to members starts with simple actions, such as answering the telephone, and ends with something as complicated as restructuring the association in response to changes in the members' environment. Members may not renew simply because they didn't get a call back when promised. More likely, however, the decision is cumulative. It results after members have made a mental list of incorrect answers, no responses at all, or having the phone ring 10 times before anyone even listens to their request. On top of that, perhaps add an annual conference that didn't deliver what the promotional materials promised or a monthly publication that misses the mark with the member. When the dues invoice arrives, members may not question "Should I renew?" but rather "Why did I join in the first place?"

Beyond answering telephones, it's necessary to get to the heart of retention: delivering the goods. What does the latest research show your members want? How is the organization responding? If something is getting in the way of a timely and effective response, can anything be done to improve the situation?

Continuum of Contact

The continuum illustrated below is by no means exhaustive, but it does suggest the variety and intensity of member contacts that occur in associations. Below it you'll find descriptions of the various contacts (ranging from personal to impersonal in intensity).

Personal ... Impersonal

Face-to-Face   Telephone   Electronic Mail   Fax   Mail   Publication

Face-to-face

• Personal meeting in the member's office

• Personal meeting at a chapter event

• Personal meeting at a national conference

Telephone

• Personal telephone call by known person (volunteer, staff member)

• Personal telephone call by unknown volunteer/staff

• Volunteer telemarketing

• Contract telemarketing

• Voice mail

Electronic Mail

• By known volunteer, staff

• By unknown volunteer, staff

Fax

• From known volunteer, staff

• Fax-on-demand (requested information)

continued on next pg.

- From unknown volunteer, staff
- Broadcast fax

Mail

- Personal letter
- Personalized letter (president/chair)
- Targeted mailing
- Bill insert
- Mass mailing

Publication

- Personalized edition using selective binding or ink-jet addressing
- Regional or specialty edition
- Informal newsletter (includes member news)
- Periodical

5. Involve members in the association. If a magic formula existed for keeping members, a key ingredient would certainly be the involvement of members. The deeper a member's involvement in your association's activities, the harder he or she will find it to walk away. Increasing involvement depends on translating the association's offerings into benefits that members value.

This communication objective aims to turn "them" into "us," to solidify an individual's commitment to your organization. When that happens, the exchange of value moves from money (paying dues and event fees) to time (serving on committees and so forth). When a member offers his or her time as a volunteer, then the full value of membership (especially in the form of

Building Volunteer Involvement

The National Association of Home Builders (NAHB) has developed a model for deepening members' participation in its activities. The Volunteer Involvement Process (VIP) operates on three assumptions:

1. Members have talents that can support organizational goals.

2. The relationship for building involvement is between the organization and the individual member.

3. Members enter the relationship at different levels and must be cultivated to develop in steps within the organization that build a long-term commitment.

The VIP model distinguishes among several levels of involvement, each representing a degree of use of member potential within the association. For each level, NAHB has developed a strategy to move members further along the path of involvement.

Base Members include the majority of members who are inactive, new to the association, or checkbook members. *Involvement strategy:* Profile individual members, then direct them to the activities of greatest interest.

continued on next pg.

relationships with other volunteers) usually becomes evident and the decision to renew is less likely a matter of money, more likely a matter of commitment.

Regardless of its objective, every act of communication becomes a form of delivering the goods to members. As such, every communication also affects retention. Take, for example, a direct mail piece promoting your annual conference. If received late, it could become a reason not to renew. Thus, the piece must serve two purposes: attracting people to the conference (primary) and convincing people to remain members (secondary). The more you can coordinate your communication objectives, the more effective your retention efforts will become.

Foothills Members (also known as participants) are motivated enough to attend functions on their own or access the organization some way (for example, by calling and ordering a publication). *Involvement strategy:* Observe their participation to assess interests and educate them on what the association has to offer; tell them how to get involved.

Ridge Members (also known as volunteers) are involved in formal committees and assist in the implementation of plans by taking on a small, medium, or large role. *Involvement strategy:* Give volunteers the support they need through targeted or topical training (such as recruitment training), documentation, and direct contact from senior volunteer officers.

Summit Members (also known as leaders) include senior officers and board members who set policy and maintain the vision of the organization. *Involvement strategy:* Provide broad-based leadership and association management training and encourage them to identify and cultivate emerging leaders.

Chapter 8

Structuring Membership for Retention

I n the early 1980s, 32 specialty retailers in the United States formed the International Map Dealers Association. A dozen years later, the group had attracted more than 500 members ranging from retailers to international publishers to government agencies. It also had a fast-growing European division and a new name: the International Map Trade Association. Several times during its short life, the organization has changed its board representation and membership structure.

This example illustrates how members do not represent a monolithic block. An association's structure typically changes over time to reflect the current and projected needs of its members. These needs often differ from those that led to the formation of the association.

A trade association, for example, may have its roots in a regulatory action that threatened to add burdensome requirements to an industry. A professional society may have been formed to address ethical practices within a specialty. In either case, the membership structure was probably based on responding to a specific

event or instance rather than long-term needs. At the time, all members had one common need that took precedence over their other needs and prompted them to band together. But as an association grows and its membership changes, a critical retention question emerges: Does the current organizational structure (such as the membership categories) adequately meet the needs of members today?

Traditional Approaches

The three most typical membership structures are as follows:

1. Common interest. At the heart of an association's mission you'll generally find a shared concern or activity. That common interest may range from graduating from the same college or university (alumni associations), producing a similar product (trade associations), earning a living in the same field (professional societies), sharing a religion (churches or synagogues), sharing common beliefs and concerns (business or social clubs), or working to address a prevalent social problem (philanthropies). Other individual membership organizations form around key benefits, such as the American Automobile Association and the American Association of Retired Persons. Membership might be open only to individuals or organizations or include both.

2. Geographic level. An association can start at any level; witness the growth of Mothers Against Drunk Driving, which began at the kitchen table of a mother angry about the death of her daughter. It moved to the regional level and then became a nationwide organization.

The level at which a membership group operates—whether local, state, regional, national, or international—affects the delivery of benefits to members. A member may be interested in publications produced at the international level but joins primarily for networks at the state or regional level. Or a member may not be able to attend nationwide annual conferences yet still appreciate the benefits of local meetings. Access, especially to meetings that are fairly close by, may make tangible that otherwise intangible sense of belonging to a national or international organization. (Remember, access includes the *perception* of being able to participate—often an important factor in the retention decision.)

Geography may also influence the membership structure known as a federation—a group of associations, each with its own constitution, bylaws, and members, that forms an umbrella organization. Federations can provide local organizations with national and international access while offering local channels of distribution to large organizations.

3. Direct/indirect. Direct members, often referred to as regular members, are directly concerned with the association's common interest. Indirect members are most often suppliers whose market includes the association's direct members. Their reason for joining is to gain access to the market, and they're usually referred to as associate, vendor, affiliate, or supporting members.

Associations with an indirect membership category report that vendors are often willing to get involved beyond paying dues by partnering with them on projects designed to support the industry, profession, or cause. Associate members are frequently some of the most effective membership recruiters because, ironically, they often have the most day-to-day contact with current members as well as prospects. Plus, savvy suppliers often spot trends and can pinpoint changes in member needs.

Even associations that don't have a formal membership category for vendors (such as some professional societies in the areas of law and medicine) may receive significant financial support from this group through advertising, exhibits, and sponsorships. Although not the primary retention concern, vendors certainly represent an important revenue source for most associations. Consequently, ensure your strategic retention planning addresses suppliers to the industry or profession whether or not they're dues-paying members.

In addition, the category of indirect members includes "users," those who aren't members but use one or more association products (such as subscribing to the monthly publication or attending an educational seminar). Sometimes you can recruit members from this group; other times, they may not be eligible. To join the American Immigration Lawyers Association (AILA), for example, members must have passed a bar exam. Many church groups have become involved in helping immigrants, but their members may not have the professional credentials to join AILA. Still, they find the associations' materials and meetings of value in their work.

Providing such user groups with adequate customer service to keep them coming back will boost your retention efforts. They not only can generate significant revenues but also may prove to be excellent membership prospects.

Catering to specialized interests

In addition to these three traditional approaches, further segmentation of membership has been occurring for a long time. It has paralleled the increasingly targeted approaches of business in general. Just as food companies have introduced different flavored versions of a flagship brand, so have associations extended their "product line" to include subcategories of membership known as **special interest groups** (SIGs for short).

SIGs—sometimes referred to as divisions, specialties, sections, or councils—offer members the opportunity to be with others like themselves and not feel lost in the crowd of the entire membership. Through the groups, members can focus on a specialty or emerging trend within the industry or profession, approach situations from a different perspective (such as large size versus small size), or network with colleagues with the same experience level or functional responsibilities. The groups provide a home for members who want to share specialized information and interests while still benefitting from the overall association's credibility and offerings.

Because they're based on narrow interests or activities, SIGs are valuable components of any retention effort. They provide key networking opportunities, programs, and products that help members perceive that the association as a whole is tailored to meeting their needs. Some SIGs operate as an "association within an association" with their own officers, governing boards, and committees. This model gives more members the opportunity to become actively involved as well as provides a training ground for future leaders of the association.

As important as they are, however, SIGs represent one large risk from a retention perspective. Members who become heavily involved in the specialized groups may come to feel they've lost their ties to the entire association and leave to form a competing group. With them they may take part of the association's membership. To avoid such problems, establish a clearly defined and strong coordinating process with your association's SIGs. That may mean providing staff to coordinate the groups or requiring volunteer leaders to meet certain requirements, such as serving on a special board.

At-risk categories

An analysis of retention rates among membership categories, both traditional and nontraditional, will generally point out the factors or characteristics that make members "at risk" for not renewing. By reviewing your association's historical files, for example, you'll be able to track when and how retention rates for a special segment or users group correlate with the average retention rate for the whole association or when they vary widely. Then, through research, you can zero in on the specific factors responsible for the discrepancy.

By far, new members represent the best-known group of at-risk members (See Chapter 9 for an in-depth discussion of their special needs). In addition, other groups may require re-evaluation and modifications of procedures, products, and services if you hope to retain them. Here are two examples of generic types. The key is to identify which are the at-risk groups in your association.

• **International members.** (In this usage, international refers to countries other than the United States). As the global marketplace has expanded, many U.S.-based associations have positioned themselves as international organizations. Attracting and retaining members in other countries, however, goes far beyond changing the name of your association to include the word "international." Special issues arise, such as the hours of phone coverage, differences in language, and even the difference between the standard size of paper in the United States (8 x 11) and in Europe (A4 paper is slightly longer).

Another classic example concerns how mail is handled. As a membership director of a large professional association noted, "My CEO wondered why we lost our international members almost as soon as we got them. I discovered, to my surprise, that our international members received only the pieces we mailed first class. Then I found out that the only thing we mailed first class was the dues renewal! Not one had ever complained. They just dropped their memberships."

As with domestic members, little things mean a lot to international members. Those outside the United States may perceive (sometimes accurately) that an organization is international in name only. It's difficult for any member to feel valued when the announcement of a conference arrives after the event, especially when this happens repeatedly.

International members have special needs. If your association truly wishes to integrate them into its structure—and retain them—you'll need to evaluate and address those needs. For instance, what can you do to make international visitors feel welcome at a U.S. conference? What currencies do you accept as payment for products and services? Have you looked into electronic technologies that pay no attention to time zones or accents? Do you charge more to send materials outside the United States? (Some U.S.-based associations waive the surcharge on international mailings to even the dues-paying field. They determined that members shouldn't be penalized for living abroad when they don't benefit from some domestic activities funded by their dues, such as lobbying or a public service campaign on American television.)

• **Student members.** Like many groups, the American Academy of Family Physicians has found student memberships an effective tool for recruiting future members into the association as well as into the medical specialty. Signing up members early on can increase their lifetime value and can justify subsidizing student memberships (setting dues below the cost of providing services). From a retention standpoint, students often appreciate the opportunity to meet with members (who may be prospective employers), and members may like the idea of mentoring up-and-coming leaders of the industry or profession.

Ideally, students will bridge over to regular membership upon graduation. To encourage that, some associations have developed programs for recent graduates, such as offering free or inexpensive insurance or membership dues that increase along with years of experience in a field. Moving students to full member status by providing more benefits that they'll value is clearly a retention strategy rather than a recruitment tactic.

No More Books

The idea behind the Young Dentist Transition Program was to shift student members of the American Dental Association (ADA) into full and active members. Originally it emphasized reading material—until ADA discovered that the last thing students wanted during their last few months of school was more to read. "Subsequent informal discussions with senior dental students and recent graduates suggested that students were eager to talk to young dentists who had just experienced what they, the students, were going through," explained Judith R. Schaefer, writing in *ASAE Membership Marketer*.

The research results prompted ADA to revamp its approach. The kit full of written materials was replaced by a live program featuring volunteers in their early years of dental practice. The ADA members, usually alumni, return to dental schools to talk with graduating seniors about the challenges they'll soon face.

Just checking

All members pay their dues. Beyond that, you'll find a range of involvement within all categories or specialized segments. Based on the long-standing assumption that the more a member is involved the more likely that member is to renew, you can chart a loyalty ladder for involvement in your association. Many of your retention efforts can be targeted to people on specific rungs on the ladder and be guided by the as-you-give-so-shall-you-receive theory. In other words, members get out of an organization what they put into it.

This conventional wisdom certainly applies to any member with the slightest desire to become an active participant. It doesn't, however, hold true for **checkbook members**. They command attention not for their level of involvement (which is minimal) but for their sheer numbers (they usually represent the majority of members in most associations).

The Loyalty Ladder

Here's an adaptation of the loyalty ladder by Raphel and Raphel, with the focus on building loyalty to the association. Ideally, members continue to move up the ladder during the lifetime of their membership rather than staying on the same rung:

• **Users.** Nonmembers who purchase products and services. Some may be membership prospects. Others are either not eligible for or interested in joining your association, but they may continue to purchase its products and services.

• **Prospects.** Potential members who meet the criteria for membership in your association. Users often represent the largest pool of prospects.

• **New Members.** Often trial members, especially if they joined under a discount membership program. New members generally have a lower retention rate than the overall membership.

• **Checkbook Members.** Existing members who send in their dues checks and purchase some products and services but otherwise rarely participate in the association. They generally represent the majority of members.

• **Participating Members.** Existing members who heavily use and purchase a variety of association products and services.

• **Partners.** The members most involved in the association, through volunteering, recruiting new members, or holding office.

These members initially join in order to receive a publication, support a cause or legislative action, obtain a specialized product (such as a professional designation or insurance program), or simply list an affiliation on their resume. That's all they want from the association. In turn, they'll pull out their checkbook once a year to send in their dues—but you probably won't hear from most of them again until the next renewal date.

As long as your association can verify that it's giving checkbook members what they want, it will retain them as satisfied members. This can be tricky. After all, how do you obtain feedback from members who don't want to actively participate in the association? In response, some associations have developed new products targeted toward members who can increase their participation without leaving their offices or homes; these include self-study courses, peer directories, and e-mail systems.

Checkbook members are an example of just one group that may have lower-than average retention rates and require special attention. Only by analyzing your membership files can you identify groups with the highest loss rates—a crucial step in designing an effective retention strategy. Here are examples of other issues to analyze:

• **Size.** Are smaller companies or larger companies more apt to drop out?

• **Experience or expertise.** Do you see an exodus among senior members, student members, or those in a special interest group?

• **Products or services purchased.** Are members who tried a new but unsuccessful product the drop-outs? Or are those who joined at your last annual conference most at risk?

• **Recruitment techniques.** Compared to members recruited by personal contact or telephone calls, are those who responded to a direct mail campaign more likely to leave?

Your association probably will have unique factors to consider as well. Once you've identified the various membership segments, you might find it helpful to develop a product grid that illustrates how well your association serves a particular group. This tool may help you identify why some members are more at risk than others for not renewing—you may have little of value to offer them.

Targeted Offerings

Here's an example of a simple Member Segment/Product Grid. It examines which segments of the membership use—and therefore value—various association products and services. Consider using such a grid to focus on an existing category of membership (student, vendor, regular member) or membership segment (international SIGs, checkbook). The key is to see what you have to offer from the targeted group member's perspective. Instead of the generic categories (interaction, information and service) you can substitute specific products/services as well as more narrowly defined member segments. This is often most useful to do with segments most at risk for retention and for new markets or segments into which the association wants to expand.

MEMBER SEGMENT/PRODUCT GRID

		PRODUCTS		
		Interaction	Information	Service
MEMBER SEGMENT	New	New Member Breakfast	New Member Newsletter	Job Bank
	Existing	Monthly Lunch	Monthly Newsletter	Insurance
	Senior	(Nothing Offered)	Quarterly Senior Newsletter	Recruitment Planning Seminar

Chapter 9

New Members: Handle With Care

An interesting paradox surrounds first-year members. While the first year of membership offers the best opportunity to lay the foundation for long-term loyalty to the association, it's also the year that members are most likely to leave the association.

In general, first-year members register the lowest retention rates of any membership category. In fact, some associations report that more than 50 percent of first-year members don't return for a second year. The percentage may also vary widely from one year to the next depending on recruitment methods and follow-up activities geared toward this group.

This situation, while serious, is hardly new. In the mid-1980s, for example, the American College of Health Care Administrators (ACHCA) discovered that its retention rate for fellows (the most senior category of members)

myth 11

Just send the new member a kit.

reality

The kit is just one part of the special handling of new members. Paying special attention to new members can convert them into lifetime members.

was 93 percent and for "actives" (members for at least two years) 90 percent. Among first-year members, however, retention dropped dramatically—down to 70 percent. ACHCA recognized the need to focus more on new members, who felt they weren't receiving personal attention. Some associations haven't come to the same realization yet; as a result, turnover among their new members remains high.

Engaging activities

A classic example of what drives new members away is the social hour preceding a luncheon or conference event. In the worst-case scenario, no one makes an attempt to meet or engage the new member in conversation. He or she is left standing against the wall, mineral-water-with-a-twist in hand, feeling left out as everyone else socializes and networks. Waiting uncomfortably for the meal to begin, the new member decides joining your association wasn't such a good idea after all.

Knowing no one is not a frivolous excuse for not attending an event. It comes up again and again, in all types of associations, when new members explain their lack of involvement. Even in a focus group of corporate attorneys—presumably not a group lacking in self-confidence—some said they hadn't attended meetings of their specialty association because they didn't want to walk into a room full of strangers.

Here are some tips on how some associations alleviate this stressful situation and make their new members feel welcome:

• **Use color coding** or a ribbon on name tags to identify new members—then ensure officers make it a priority to focus on these people and make introductions while "doing the rounds."

• **Set up a hospitality committee** to oversee a buddy system that pairs a veteran member with a new member for the event. The buddy might even call the new member in advance. This system not only can boost attendance at meetings but also help retain senior members who like to feel valued.

• **Hold a reception** or orientation for new members before the program begins. This enables new members to meet one another and elected leaders and ensures they won't be alone at the meeting that follows. This is also a good opportunity for committee chairs to talk about their upcoming activities (and perhaps recruit some volunteers).

• **Have an ice breaker.** One association, for example, appoints one of its new members to hand out cash to the fifth (or tenth, or whatever) person who introduces himself or herself during the networking session that precedes the program. As you might imagine, this practice makes new members very popular with existing members. The money is only a token, perhaps $25, but it motivates current members to speak to newcomers and establishes introductory conversations as the norm at the association's events.

As engaging and effective as these activities may be, what happens when the event concludes? Days, even weeks, may go by with no contact from the association other than an impersonal newsletter, a meeting announcement, or a journal showing up in the mail. The once enthusiastic new member sinks back into the nameless, faceless existence of "Memberland." If this situation persists for the remainder of the membership year, the new member will find it easy to ignore all your association's mailings—notably the renewal invoice. But if your association takes the right actions, it can convert first-year members into life-long members.

High Signs

To keep members past the first year, associations need to focus on three actions: *High Touch* (contact), *High Active* (participation), and *High Inform* (communication). Together they form the foundation upon which new members build a personal connection with the association, which in turn leads to their perception of value. Most associations do some of each, but they don't always perform these essential actions in a systematic way and at the necessary intensity.

myth 12

Retention begins the moment a member joins.

reality

Retention is tied in part to how a member was recruited; it starts with the first contact, even before joining.

• **High Touch.** Unless the new member has a high internal motivation for joining (such as needing a certification offered only by the association), he or she will often need assistance in understanding and taking full advantage of their membership.

Initial contact refers to both the first time a member interacts in any way with the association and to the first substantive contact. Often both happen simultaneously. Because the old cliche holds true—you never get a second chance to make a first impression—you'll want to ensure that the first contact is positive.

Why Do Members Join?

Based on several studies, the most common reasons that people give for joining an association are to:

- Receive the association's publications to keep up-to-date.

- Participate in educational opportunities, such as the annual conference, topical meetings, trade show, or training for certification or accreditation.

- Get cutting-edge information and feedback from peers through networking.

- Obtain benefits (either unique to a particular association or generic) such as discounts for car rentals or insurance programs.

- Support the association's lobbying or political action efforts.

- Receive a professional designation; increase professional or personal status.

- Access the association's membership directory, job bank, or networking events to locate a new job or new clients.

- Support the mission, cause, or values of the association.

- Get involved in a leadership capacity to gain status or to contribute to the profession or industry.

- Please someone else (boss, client, peers).

- Compare the association to another that they're considering joining or already belong to.

Obviously, both the order as well as the reasons will vary from association to association.

At the same time, however, guard against creating expectations that the association may find impossible to satisfy. Overeager volunteers or commissioned telemarketers, for example, might raise unrealistic expectations during the recruiting process. If those expectations are not adjusted early on, you're likely to have an unsatisfied member on your hands when renewal time arrives.

To identify what a new member expects, consider having a knowledgeable staff member or volunteer call to extend a welcome to the association and verify that basic information is correct. Or go a step further and have a trained caller discuss expectations with the new member. In any case, the question to be answered is "Why did you join?" Most members have a specific reason for joining and will gladly share it. Obviously, this is also the time to correct any false expectations so the relationship with the member gets off to a good start.

A phone call or personal visit becomes especially important when the new member has been recruited through a direct mail campaign. The personal contact emphasizes that your association is composed of people; it's not a faceless, voiceless, monolithic organization. Since you can't be sure new members have ever looked at their membership kit, a one-on-one conversation can guide the new recruit to undiscovered products or services.

"When the director of membership services first suggested calling new members, I am embarrassed to admit I was against it as a waste of staff time and resources," reports the CEO of a state trade association. "She finally convinced me to try it with a test group and control group of new members. One group got calls, the other didn't. It was so successful that after the first year all new members started getting quarterly calls. Now I ask why we didn't do it sooner. All those lost members and dollars!" To handle the calls the association hired another staff person, whose salary is more than covered by the increased number of renewals.

This initial contact should occur within a few days of your receipt of the member's application. Even calling just to say "Thank you. We've received your application," lets members know your association values them and can set the stage for lifetime loyalty. In the absence of a call or personal visit, at least send a postcard or letter that acknowledges receipt of the new member's application and indicates association materials are on their way.

Six-Month Checkup

After the enthusiasm of orientation has faded—and before the renewal notice arrives—new members can feel neglected. A telephone contact program such as the one outlined below can ensure that your association builds a positive relationship with new members.

Four months into membership, a volunteer or staff member calls to review the benefits available. "Just checking to see how you're doing and if you had any questions. What association products have you used? Are there any others you are interested in? . . . Let me tell you about them in greater detail. By the way, the event this month will be . . ."

Month five brings another telephone call, this time to prepare for an upcoming survey: "Just calling to let you know that we'll be sending a brief survey next month to get your impressions after the first six months of membership. Do you have any questions? By the way, we have a new product coming out this month . . ."

At the **six-month** mark, the survey is mailed and followed by a telephone call a week later: "Have you received the six-month survey? It's really important to us to know how you are doing. By the way, this month . . ."

At **month seven**, someone calls to either thank the member for returning the survey or remind them of the survey's importance: "Thanks so much for sending in your survey so promptly. It will really help us serve you better. Any questions about the survey? By the way, this month . . ."

At **eight months**, the check-in includes a push for involvement: "I know we've talked about some of the benefits you've found most useful over the last few months. Now that you've been a member for seven months, are there ways you'd like to get *more* involved? Don't forget that this month . . ."

Month nine focuses on the positive experiences the member has had during the year and prepares him or her for renewal: "It's hard to believe how fast this year has gone by. I hope you've found some useful benefits. The first year is always a good time to explore, and in the second year you can focus more on certain events or programs. Speaking of which, don't forget . . ."

Ongoing contact, the other component of a high-touch strategy, comes into play after the first three months of orientation materials and activities have concluded. As Elizabeth Pomeroy notes in *Attracting, Organizing & Keeping Members*, the middle six months of the first year are ideal for a "carefully planned flow of materials and invitations, blended with contact with other members to educate and involve the new member quickly." Whatever schedule of contacts you establish, ensure they allow new members ample opportunity to ask questions and to understand that the association is making every effort to respond to their needs.

• **High Active.** In the course of making and maintaining contact, you should also attempt to draw the member into participating in the association. The more actively engaged new members are, the greater the chance they'll recognize the value of the association to them personally. That recognition is a key ingredient to retention.

At the First Convention

Attending a convention where you don't know a soul doesn't have to be an intimidating experience. Here's how the Society for Foodservice Management (SFM) has handled new members at its annual conference since 1989.

Greeters, usually members of the conference organizing committees, work in pairs to greet new members during registration and chat with them for a few minutes. Committee members, together with SFM past presidents, also serve as *buddies* to a maximum of three new members (who each wear a "New Kid on the Block" button). In turn, each buddy wears an "I'm a Buddy" badge and accompanies new members to select events.

With their registration materials, all first-time attendees also receive instructions on playing *The Board Game*. The goal is for each new member to meet all the association's directors and officers—pictured in an accompanying booklet—and obtain their signatures. Everyone turning in a completed booklet becomes eligible for a special prize drawing.

Many people, for example, join an association for networking. But just telling them about networking events isn't enough. You'll need to encourage them to attend and then introduce them to others when they do. Consider establishing a partnering program that matches ambassadors, buddies, mentors, and sponsors—or whatever name you choose to give veteran members—with new members as a start on their network.

If you signed up the new member through a member-get-a-member campaign, the recruiter is a natural choice as a partner. In fact, some associations have extended their member-get-a-member campaigns to include bonus credit for *retaining* members. Likewise, you might offer a retention bonus to telemarketers on top of a recruitment commission. This underscores the close ties between recruitment and retention—and gives the recruiter additional incentive to recruit properly and to keep in touch with the members they sign up. (Plus, experienced members often enjoy serving as a mentor or "guide" to the association, and the opportunity to provide that assistance may factor into their own renewal decision.)

Another form of participation is use of your association's products. To encourage this, many associations offer coupon booklets to new members that include special offers such as "Your first monthly luncheon is free" or "15 percent off your first order of publications." Other options include designing products specifically for new members (such as a newsletter or program) or offering a sliding dues scale based on years in the field. Although your association essentially subsidizes these product trial usages, new members may eventually become regular buyers. But most important to retention, the member who is engaged in using a variety of products is more likely to renew.

Whatever method you use, the goal of "high active" remains the same: Ensuring that new members are invited to try the association products and become active in committees and events. Then they'll feel they're getting value.

• **High Inform**. In addition to the standard newsletters, promotions, and mailings that all members receive, new members may require specialized information to get up to speed on what your association has to offer.

The centerpiece of "high inform" efforts is typically the new-member kit. As the primary reference source on the association, the kit commonly contains a list of benefits, list of staff contacts, directory of available services,

Welcome Aboard

In its *Retention Strategies Kit* developed for state affiliates, the National Association of Professional Insurance Agents outlines these procedures for welcoming new members:

- Acknowledge receipt of a new member's application immediately. People assume that signing the application immediately makes them a member, so don't delay the welcome letter and new member kit. If processing takes a while, send a welcome postcard or give them a call alerting them to the imminent arrival of the kit.

- Don't overwhelm the new member with too many materials at once. The average member doesn't read everything and may not save the information for future reference. If you have a lot of welcome materials, consider sending them in several installments. Or, provide a checklist of services and programs and include a "request for more information" form.

- Send a personalized letter of welcome signed by the president or membership chair.

- Remove the new member's name from the prospect list.

- Welcome members and prospects at association functions, perhaps by assigning a volunteer or staff member to greet participants at the door.

- If members are too spread out geographically to conduct orientation meetings, ask a volunteer in the area to pay a visit to the new member.

sample newsletter(s) or journal(s), and product list or catalog. Based on feedback from new members, choose the contents to address common needs and, above all, to be *useful*.

For instance, research by the Association for Corporate Computing Technical Professionals (ACCTP) showed that members often collected its

A Year-Long Effort

The National Association of Home Builders' (NAHB) *Retention Handbook* advises "communicating frequently and thoroughly with new members throughout the entire year, making sure they feel welcome and important." Specifically, NAHB recommends the following:

• Assign an ambassador to each new member. Ambassadors can reinforce the new member's decision to join by answering questions about association services, inviting him or her to become involved in association activities, and offering personal testimony about the organization's value.

• Create a newsletter or bulletin just for new members. Explain how to use a particular association program and describe the benefit received. Feature an in-depth profile of a different committee or council in each issue, emphasizing how its members have profited from their involvement.

• Emphasize recent association accomplishments in a personal letter from the association president. Send it to all new members six months into their membership.

• Let members know their opinions and ideas are welcome. Publish the names and phone numbers of association leaders. Early in the first year, send a questionnaire asking new members about their satisfaction with association services.

• Target high-risk renewals. Maintain a database showing what activities new members have participated in. Administer TLC to those who've never participated—otherwise, they'll be the first to leave.

monthly magazines in binders and used them as a complement to computer manuals. The association recast its membership kit into a three-hole-punched format to encourage new members to keep membership materials as close at hand as the magazines.

In your zeal for showing new members all the association has to offer, however, you risk overwhelming them. In some associations, for example, the new-member kit is referred to (appropriately) as "the hernia kit" because it contains several pounds of paper. You might find it more effective to divide the kit's contents and send them in segments, as a planned flow of materials over time. Ideally, this flow should begin immediately after the initial contact of a postcard, call, or face-to-face visit. The longer you wait, the further you reduce the first-year window of opportunity for proving the association's value to the new member. That can be an expensive delay, a costly mistake from a retention perspective.

Imagine the frustration of joining an association and having to wait *three months* before receiving any materials. That happened to be the case in one state association, where the new CEO asked staff to treat him as a new member. "I found that it took three months to get our monthly journal," he reports. "It turned out to be an administrative problem because our labels came from national, even though members joined at the state level." The CEO couldn't change the national's procedures, but he did suggest making temporary labels before forwarding applications to the national organization. The state group could then send new members all mailings before they were officially added to the national's list.

Sealing the Deal

If the first year was a positive experience and resulted in renewal, then the second year can lead the member into a lifelong membership. Special handling of second-year members may still be merited as you integrate them more fully into the association through additional responsibilities.

According to a longstanding rule of thumb, 20 percent of members do 80 percent of the volunteering. This won't necessarily be the case in the future. Given increased time pressures and continued staff reductions, volunteers are already harder to attract yet needed more than ever. Philanthropic organizations in particular have found it easier to get members to give money rather than their time.

Be Alert to Other Factors

In addition to cherrypicking members (See Chapter 5), be on the lookout for these special situations that can affect retention:

• **Institutional or corporate members** typically appoint a key contact person or representative to the association. Over time, this person may change, and his or her successor may know little about your association. You may find it helpful to treat the new contact as a new member even if the organization has been a member for decades. It's important to reinforce the value of the association to this person, who may be responsible for the renewal decision.

• **Bargain memberships** refer to special offers such as half-year "trial" memberships, free memberships, or other types of discounts to a select pool of prospects. The American Bar Association, for example, provides a free year of membership to new attorneys when they pass the bar exam. These offers can further increase your association's cost for new members.

The theory behind these subsidized approaches is that the association spreads out the new-member costs, which can exceed the first year's dues, over the lifetime of membership. But that's assuming most members recruited this way will renew. In fact, bargain memberships usually have a higher attrition rate because members weren't required to make a full monetary investment and consequently are less committed to the association. Some associations have decided bargain memberships erode the value of membership and have discontinued them. Certainly, special offers can attract a large number of members for one year. But only by tracking the correlation between recruitment methods and retention rates will you know which approach is worthwhile to your association in the long run.

This situation has prompted many organizations to involve more members with each doing less, to form more committees and subcommittees with each having a narrower responsibility. Fortunately, this approach fits well with second-year members. They can accept responsibility, yet its narrow focus won't overwhelm them as they continue to learn about all the association has to offer.

Whether you're focusing on first- or second-year members, take the time to find out what each member wants from his or her association. When you know what new members expect, you can connect them with the appropriate people and resources. And when new members feel they're getting a lot out of the association, they'll dive in deeper in terms of participation and commitment to remaining a member for years to come.

Chapter 10

The Strategic Retention Team

To be most effective, the strategic retention effort needs the CEO's initiative, vision, and leadership. Yet the CEO can't do the job alone. Supporting and implementing his or her efforts are three key groups: volunteers, paid staff, and in particular the membership department. All have important roles to play in building and maintaining a retention-oriented culture throughout the association.

The Volunteer Role

Membership brochures can list numerous benefits of belonging to your association. But no one can provide a better testimony about the value of membership than an active volunteer who has personally experienced that value. In addition, articulating the benefits of membership to prospects or new members helps reinforce for existing members why they belong to the association.

Many associations report that it is increasingly hard to recruit volunteers. Those who previously sought volunteer experience as a way to develop skills or achieve recognition seem to be shrinking in numbers. Members report that either their jobs have become more demanding or they want to spend more time on personal needs such as families. Also, member expectations have changed; volunteers want to know what the association can do for them, rather than vice versa.

> **"I realized that many of my staff did not have the faintest idea of what our members really do. We initiated some field trips and I placed some of my senior, key personnel on short details with some of our members. It has made a big difference in my staff's understanding of the needs and pressures my members are under."**
>
> —*CEO Focus Group Participant*

As previously discussed, the deeper a member's involvement, the harder he or she will find it to ignore your next dues notice (See Chapter 7). Turning members into volunteers can help ensure they not only assist with your retention efforts but also renew their own memberships. A growing number of associations report they need to proactively recruit volunteers from their inactive members, their pool of untapped talent. Association executives participating in our research suggest the following:

• **Emphasize the benefits of volunteering.** Leadership training programs often focus on management skills such as running a meeting and parliamentary procedure. But volunteers can also develop broader skills, such as public speaking, delegating, and organizing. Also point out that volunteers can learn or enhance skills they might not have the opportunity to do in their jobs, such as producing a publication or planning a program. These can foster personal and professional growth and enhance a resume.

• **Provide training for working with other volunteers.** Some officers and committee chairs expect a lot from rank-and-file members who are less committed than they. Addressing—and, in some cases, adjusting—expectations through training among both types of volunteers can head off frustrations that may develop and fuel the non-renewal decision.

• **Prepare volunteer job descriptions.** Position descriptions should clearly define the commitment expected of volunteers, especially those at the officer and board level.

• **Tap the talents of retired members and past officers.** The American Bankers Association, for instance, asks retired bankers to make on-site personal visits to members and prospects.

• **Integrate several types of volunteers into the retention process.** While the top elected volunteers, generally the board of directors, take a leadership role in retention, they are not necessarily representative of rank-and-file members. They may be older, more educated, or from larger organizations that support their time commitment to the association. As a result, leaders may bring a different perspective to membership issues. In some cases, associations are establishing seats on their boards for certain under-represented segments such as smaller companies or younger members.

As the CEO of a national trade association explains, "The board is probably the worst representative group because they know too much. They need to understand things from the rank-and-file members. If members are honest with them, it serves as an early warning system and gives the board a sense

Not a Winning Idea

The danger of not including various perspectives among volunteer leaders became clear in one trade association. Its board proposed a new dues structure based on the "country club model." The association would assess each member company an amount to spend on non-dues purchases based on their level of dues. If, for example, a company paid $5,000 in annual dues, the association expected it to spend an additional $1,000 on seminars, publications, conferences, and other products and programs. If the corporate membership dues were $10,000, the assessment would be $2,000, and so forth. If members failed to spend the assessed amount, they'd be billed for the difference.

Most of the board members represented the largest and most active members and always spent well over the targeted amounts. They didn't see any problems with the proposal. A staff member, however, recommended testing the proposal through a series of six focus groups in three cities.

Upon hearing the proposal in the focus groups, the rank-and-file members became outraged. Several participants said they'd quit the association if the plan were adopted. Most of the board immediately reconsidered; a few who didn't believe the results called some members on their own and found the focus groups had been right on target. The idea, rather than the association, died a quick death.

of the problems staff face." This small association asks its board members to divide up and call all members once a year to ensure the board doesn't become too isolated.

Your membership committee or task force can provide the perspective that may be missing on the board. Formed at any level, from local to international, such a group typically gives input to the board and may implement new-member activities as well as recruitment and retention campaigns. For many associations, the membership committee is the first line of success

Inviting Involvement

This invitation to volunteer, written by Leslie Shields, is excerpted from a newsletter published by the Washington, D.C., chapter of the American Society for Training & Development:

"We have projects for those who need serious stimulation and projects for those who need humor and fun. Our projects can be as short as one hour or as long as eight hours. You can work alone or be part of a team. Not sure about what we have? Here's a partial listing of how you can be involved in the chapter:"

- Provide links to other professional organizations.
- Identify speakers for monthly meetings and other chapter events.
- Take photographs of chapter activities.
- Provide desktop publishing services.
- Write an article for the newsletter.
- Assist with planning programs.
- Greet new members.
- Raise funds for scholarships.
- Start a special interest group.
- Serve on a committee.
- Represent the chapter at conferences.
- Help with registration.
- Provide guidance to other members.
- Facilitate programs.

when it comes to making contact with those most likely not to renew—new members. Research on such topics as price sensitivity and dues increases help avoid board decisions that don't reflect the view of the membership.

• **Recognize volunteers' contributions.** In addition to thanking members at meetings and in publications, let their employers (especially supervisors) know of their contributions to the profession, industry, or community. Other associations even invite the volunteers' families to a recognition event. The thanks can come from the top volunteer or from the professional staff—what matters is that it happens.

Staff—on the Front Lines

"Staff learn in three ways: by example, by example, and by example. If the CEO doesn't return phone calls, the staff won't return calls. If the CEO takes three weeks to answer a letter, so will the staff." This observation, from a state association's chief staff executive, emphasizes the CEO's role in setting the tone for and demonstrating a commitment to retention as a strategic process.

The paid staff affects membership retention every day through their interactions with members. And those interactions typically follow the style set by the CEO. If he or she delegates retention and never gives it another thought, the rest of the staff will do the same.

Keeping members can become complicated if the organizational structure includes city-, county-, regional-, or state-based membership units—usually called chapters or affiliates. Then you also may be working with volunteers and sometimes paid staff at multiple levels. Like the conflicts that erupt between the headquarters and field offices of corporations, tensions among national or international associations and their chapters can escalate into a "we versus they" attitude. Chapter members are likely to say, "Our unit is different from all the others; our members have different needs" and ask, "What am I getting for my money from headquarters?" The national organization, on the other hand, probably wonders, "Why doesn't this chapter realize everything we do for it?" Meanwhile, the individual member just wants to know the answer to "Should I renew?"

To avoid these conflicts, each level needs a clear understanding of its specific roles and responsibilities in meeting member needs. In addition, all membership units must know how they work together as a team to meet

The Daily Grind

If you think your staff doesn't have the foggiest idea what your members do, consider launching a program that lets them find out first hand. That's what the National Association of College Stores (NACS) did by sending all staff—including the CEO—to work alongside members during peak business periods. The staff not only experienced "real life" from the member's perspective but also had the opportunity to get to know individual members better.

In addition, staff members developed a better appreciation for the challenges facing NACS members and zeroed in on unmet needs that had been previously unidentified. NACS now asks all new staff members to spend some time working in a member's operation.

members' needs with membership retention as their common goal. The American Academy of Family Physicians (AAFP) achieved both of these objectives when it restructured its membership classifications. As part of a three-year membership marketing plan, AAFP asked its chapters to cross-reference various lists of physicians. In turn, for expending that effort, the national office assured chapters that it would retain all the names on computer files; never again would chapters have to maintain manual prospect lists.

What if AAFP had not been able to work out the conflict and the national office had implemented the recruitment and retention program on its own? What if the conflict ended up being played out in front of every member? Then the individual member would no doubt have received mixed messages. The national publications would have been promoting a program that the local chapter might never have mentioned in its newsletters and meetings, leading the member to question the association's ability to use dues dollars effectively to communicate and get things done.

Other groups, including the Building Owners and Managers Association International and the National Association of Professional Insurance Agents, have designed retention kits at the national level for use by the field organizations. These materials may offer one master model or several alternatives for the membership unit to implement based on members' needs. Regardless of the method(s) suggested, the kits encourage a partnership and coordination among multiple membership levels.

"The" Job

While retention is part of everyone's job, it is *the* job for the membership staff. The organization and duties of the membership function vary considerably among associations. Some route all calls from members to a customer service center that answers membership questions, processes publication orders, and handles complaints and compliments. Some associations designate the membership staff as the primary contact for any research on members, products, and services. In others, however, the membership unit has responsibility primarily for clerical functions such as updating member records and sending out dues notices on time. These clerical functions don't reflect the role that marketing plays in retention.

Whereas marketing and recruitment have long been partners in many associations, marketing and retention—where the focus is on the current member—aren't always related. Significant effort goes into explaining the benefits of an association to potential members; these same benefits need to be repeated to the members you want to retain. Research on current as well as prospective members will yield insights into the mix of products and services the association must develop to meet the current and future needs of members.

A great danger to any membership organization is for the non-membership staff and volunteers to feel that "they don't do membership." Every staff member is responsible for membership, especially retention. The CEO must ensure that message becomes embedded into the association's culture, planning, and the daily activities of all staff and volunteers.

Chapter 11

Building Strategic Retention Into Your Association Plan: The Strategic Retention Audit

Strategic retention ties together all the elements of an association's strategic and operating plans. It affects every association activity from purchasing new membership software to developing the annual financial planning package to establishing this year's government affairs agenda. If these or any other association activity cannot be related to retention—to keeping members—then that activity must be seriously questioned.

To ensure that strategic retention is integrated into every element of your association's strategic and operational plans, the following concepts should be included. Keeping members requires:

• **A strategic process that's implemented daily**. Every aspect of planning must be viewed through the lens of retention. This requires looking at changes in the world from the perspective of members and figuring out how your association can help members deal with those changes. Retention should permeate every element of the association's planning and implementation.

• **The CEO's leadership, supported by staff and volunteers.** If the CEO demonstrates that retention is a priority to be addressed daily, then the staff and volunteers will follow his or her example. If the CEO relegates retention to a membership clerk, so will everyone else. It is that simple.

• **Identifying and responding to what members want.** The relationship between value and retention is straightforward: If members believe value exists, they'll retain their membership. The hard part is determining value *from the members' perspective.*

• **Purposeful communication.** Every contact should serve to identify members' wants and needs, stay in touch, inform, respond to needs, or involve members in the organization. New members (those in their first or second year of membership) require special communication efforts to help them take advantage of all your association has to offer. Any time you make contact with members, you're influencing their retention decision.

• **Moving beyond statistics.** More than the numbers associated with meeting or exceeding an arbitrary goal, retention focuses on lifetime income and lifetime value. The latter concept is particularly appropriate because it considers the time, as well as the money, that a member contributes over the course of membership.

• **Delivering the goods.** This simply means that you offer members what they want—and then make sure they get it. For one member, that might mean spelling his name correctly. For another, it might mean offering a product that she can't obtain anywhere else.

Remember the Realities

At one time, the myths surrounding retention may have been based in truth. In today's changing world, however, membership renewal isn't as automatic an action as it once was. Longstanding myths must give way to the realities of retention. The future of your association depends on responding to those realities. After all, your association's entire reason for existing is its members. As your most precious resource, your members deserve to be your primary focus. If they are, the payback could be for a lifetime.

Undertaking an Audit

As you prepare to further incorporate retention into your association's plans and processes, you might find it helpful to conduct an audit of your current operations. By systematically analyzing activities, you put the actions, products, and services of your association into another context: You see them from the perspective of the member making the renewal decision. You'll also see how all the association's actions affect that strategic retention decision.

The strategic retention audit outlined here follows the book *Keeping Members: The Myths & Realities*. The strengths and weaknesses that emerge as you answer the questions related to your strategic retention effort can highlight areas that should be integrated into or changed in your association's strategic and operational planning.

Association Strategic Retention Audit

1. Environmental Scan

- How do you see the changing world affecting what your members need from their association?
- What effects have changing organizational structures within your industry, profession, or cause had on your association membership?
- What business is your association in?
- How has your association adapted to changing member needs?
- How technologically literate is your membership? How connected is your association to the information highway?
- Who spearheads your association's strategic retention planning?
- Are any retention myths prevalent in your association?

2. Core Issues

- Where is your retention vision described? How do you ensure its implementation?
- Is retention an integrated, association-wide responsibility in your organization?
- Are you a recruitment- or a retention-focused organization?
- What are your retention patterns?
- Is churn an issue for your association?
- How do you ensure that your association is recruiting for keeps and not just for one year?
- What is the average lifetime value of a member? (Include both lifetime income, cost, and non-economic contributions such as volunteer time and recruiting.)
- How do you protect your membership cachet?

3. Numbers, Trends, and Issues

- What economic and industrial changes do you expect will affect your association in the next five years?

- What demographic or lifestyle changes do you expect will affect your association in the next five years?

- Who are your competitors? Has your relative strength (position) changed over the last five years?

- Does your association include the key organizations or individuals in your industry, profession, or cause? If not, why?

- When you analyze your retention rate (for the whole association and by key segments) over the last five years, what trends emerge? Can you explain the changes?

- What is your overall retention rate currently? Who/how do you determine a target retention rate for the upcoming year?

- What key factors affect your retention rate?

- Do any segments of your membership have lower (or higher) retention rates than the association as a whole? If so, why?

- Who pays your members' dues? Is this changing?

4. Member Satisfaction and Service

- How does your association identify member expectations?

- How satisfied are members with your association in general and its products and services in particular? How do you know?

- How do staff members and volunteer leaders deal with dissatisfied customers? Do you offer a money-back guarantee or have service standards?

- Are staff and volunteers trained in member satisfaction techniques? Is member feedback shared with them?

- How do staff and volunteers learn about the association and keep informed about its current structure, benefits, products, and services?

- How do you track complaints? Who responds to complaints? When?

- What was the last major technology change your association made for the sake of efficiency? How did the change affect members? What did members think of the change?

- Identify one major "unforseen circumstance" that occurred within the last 12 months. Describe how you dealt with it and explained it to members.

5. Evaluating Products and Services

- How well do you understand your members' perceived value of the association?

- What is the member perception of your association's brand name? How do you enhance and maintain your brand name equity?

- What products and services do you currently offer to members? Do you have a complete listing? How do you develop new products? Retire outdated products?

- Which association products and services do you bundle into the basic membership? When did you last analyze the package? How does your association evaluate how much members value these products?

- How have your members' needs changed over the last year? How have you modified existing products and developed new products to meet these needs?

- Does your association have a golden handcuff? Is it at risk from a competitor? How many members would remain if you didn't have it?

- Does your association have cherrypickers (for products or membership)? Is it a growing issue?

6. Research

- What kind of information about members can you currently obtain from existing files and databases? How have you used this information recently to help meet members' needs?

- What kind of retention research has your association conducted in the last year?

- What are some of the key findings from your most recent research?

- What are the key reasons members give for joining your association? What are their primary reasons for retaining their membership? For dropping their membership?

- What association benefits do your members value most? How do you know?

- How can your association be more responsive to members' needs?

- How can you be more effective with special segments?

- How effective is your current exit research? Can you improve it?

7. Communications

- Evaluate how well your communication program does the following:
  — Identify needs
  — Establish contact
  — Inform
  — Respond
  — Involve members

- Evaluate the effectiveness of your communication program regarding:
  — Timing
  — Frequency
  — Format (technology)
  — Audience
  — Implementation

- How does your association coordinate communications with your membership (for example, mailings from different departments)?

- Identify some of the triggering events for your association and its members.

- Are you actively exploring the use of new technologies?

8. Segmentation and Targeting

- Does your association's organizational structure adequately meet the current and projected needs of members?

- What member categories, segments, or special populations does your association include? How do you meet the needs of these subgroups?

- How are special interest groups coordinated, eliminated, or started?

- Which segments represent the greatest retention risks? How do you know?

- How do you encourage members to move up the association loyalty ladder?

- How do you ensure retention of checkbook and indirect members?

- When you fill in the member segment/product grid, are some segments underserved?

9. New and Second-Year Members

- How does your association encourage recruiting for retention rather than for one year?

- Do you track first-year retention rates based on how members were recruited? Which method is the most effective for retention?

- What is the retention rate of your association's first-year members? Second-year members? How do these rates compare to your average retention rate for the association overall?

- Describe your association's "high touch" activities aimed at first-year members.

- How do you encourage your first-year members to become active?

- Do you do anything special to keep your new members informed?

- Does your association have any special situations regarding first-year members? How do you handle them?

- What are the top five reasons first-year members give for joining your association? For dropping? Why do second-year members retain their membership?

- How do you seal the membership decision with second-year members?

10. Structuring Responsibilities

- How recently have you evaluated the effectiveness of your volunteer structure?

- If your association is multi-level, how do you enhance the partnership between different levels?

- Is the board of directors representative of your rank-and- file members? If not, how do you obtain balanced feedback?

- How does the CEO set the tone for the retention effort in your association?

- Does staff understand what business your members are in?

- What functions does your membership department cover (research, marketing, and so forth)?

- How effective is your volunteer membership committee? If you don't have one, why not?

- What training do you provide for volunteers and staff on member satisfaction and on integrating retention into everyone's job?

- Is it getting harder for your association to find volunteers? If so, why? How are you addressing the situation?

- How do you recognize and thank volunteers?

- How do you motivate inactive members to become active volunteers?

11. Planning for Retention

- How do you integrate retention into your strategic planning?

- How do you integrate retention into your operational planning?

- How do you ensure that all staff and volunteer leaders understand the importance of retention to the future of your association?

Bibliography

References Cited in the Text

Blankenship, Albert B. And George E. Breen, *State-of-the-Art Marketing Research*, American Marketing Association, Chicago, Illinois, 1993.

"Database Marketing: A Potent New Tool for Selling," *Business Week*, September 5, 1994.

Distelhorst, Garis F., "Trying on Member's Jobs," *Association Management*, January 1990, American Society of Association Executives, Washington, D.C.

Drucker, Peter F., "What Business Can Learn from Nonprofits," *Harvard Business Review*, July-August 1989.

Kotler, Philip, and Alan R. Andreasen, *Strategic Marketing for Nonprofit Organizations*, 4th ed. Prentice-Hall, Englewood Cliffs, New Jersey, 1991.

Jackson, Katie, *Retention Strategies Kit*, National Association of Professional Insurance Agents, Alexandria, Virginia, 1993.

Lang, Alexandra, "Quality—A Tale of Two Perceptions," *ASAE Membership Marketer*, August 1993, American Society of Association Executives, Washington, D.C.

Newton, Patricia M., and Ginny Thiersch, "Empowering Chapters Through Effective Communications," *The National-Chapter Partnership: A Guide for the Chapter Relations Professional*, American Society of Association Executives, Washington, D.C., 1993.

Peppers, Don, and Martha Rogers, *The One-to-One Future: Building Relationships One Customer at a Time*, Currency/Doubleday, New York, 1993.

Peters, Tom, *Thriving on Chaos: Handbook for a Management Revolution*, Harper Perennial, New York, 1991.

Playing for Keeps: Retention Handbook, National Association of Home Builders, Washington, D.C., 1991.

Pomeroy, Elizabeth R., "Membership Retention," *Attracting, Organizing & Keeping Members*, American Society of Association Executives, Washington, D.C., 1989.

Raphel, Neil and Murray Raphel, *Up the Loyalty Ladder*, Harper Collins, New York, 1995.

Rhinesmith, Kathleen L., and Arlene Farber Sirkin, "Maximizing the Use of Focus Groups in Associations," *A Sharing of Expertise and Experience*, Vol. 10, American Society of Association Executives, Washington, D.C., 1992.

Ries, Al, and Jack Trout, *Positioning: The Battle for Your Mind*, McGraw-Hill, New York, 1986.

Schaefer, Judith R., "Communicating the Value of Membership: Turning Student Members Into Professional Members," *ASAE Membership Marketer*, September 1993, American Society of Association Executives, Washington, D.C.

Shields, Leslie, "Spirit of Volunteerism," *The Torch*, March 1994, American Society of Training and Development, Washington, D.C., chapter.

Siegel, Patricia A., and James S. DeLizia, "Involving Other Members," *Leadership*, American Society of Association Executives, Washington, D.C., 1993.

Stewart, Thomas A., "Welcome to the Revolution," *Fortune*, December 1993.

Additional Resources

Able, Edward, "Future Issues and Opportunities," *Principles of Association Management*, 2nd ed., American Society of Association Executives, Washington, D.C., 1988.

Albrecht, Karl, and Laurence J. Bradford, *The Service Advantage: How to Identify and Fulfill Customer Needs*, Dow Jones-Irwin, Inc., Homewood, Illinois, 1989.

_____, and Ron Zemke, *Service America! Doing Business in the New Economy*, Dow Jones-Irwin, Inc., Homewood, Illinois, 1985.

Allen, Susan, "Special Attention to New Members Pays Off," *Association Management*, February 1986, American Society of Association Executives, Washington, D.C.

American Society of Association Executives, *A Decade of Expertise and Experience in Membership Marketing*, Washington, D.C., 1993.

_____, *Fundamentals of Association Management: Marketing*, Washington, D.C., 1983.

_____, *Selling a Dues Increase*, Washington, D.C., 1982.

Andreasen, Alan R., "Nonprofits: Check Your Attention to Customers," *Harvard Business Review*, May-June 1982.

Axelrod, Nancy R., *The Chief Executive's Role in Developing the Nonprofit Board*, National Center for Nonprofit Boards, Washington, D.C., 1988.

Ballen, Anne, "The Buddy System," *Association Management*, May 1989, American Society of Association Executives, Washington, D.C.

Barnstable, Rose, and Barbara Connell, "Key Elements of a New Member Kit," *ASAE Membership Marketer*, March 1992, American Society of Association Executives, Washington, D.C.

Brimsek, Tobi, *Inside Information: Profiles of Association Libraries and Information Centers*, Special Libraries Association, Washington, D.C., 1991.

Burke, Christine E., and Diana McCauley, "The Planning Process: More than Just Deciding What to Do," *ASAE Membership Marketer*, Distinguished Paper Series, American Society of Association Executives, Washington, D.C., June 1992.

Butler, Wilford A., "Membership Development," *Principles of Association Management*, 2nd ed., American Society of Association Executives, Washington, D.C., 1988.

Carey, Stephen C., ed. "A Marketing Bibliography for Nonprofits," Part I, *Executive Update*, April 1988, Greater Washington Society of Association Executives, Washington, D.C.

_____, ed., *Marketing the Nonprofit Association*, The Greater Washington Society of Association Executives Foundation, Washington, D.C., 1992.

Coates & Jarratt, Inc., *Managing Your Future as an Association: Thinking About Trends and Working With Their Consequences*, American Society of Association Executives, Washington, D.C., 1994.

Deutsch, Bob, "Know Your Business, and Serve Your Members Well," *ASAE Membership Marketer*, August 1993, American Society of Association Executives, Washington, D.C.

Drucker, Peter F., *The New Realities*, Harper and Row, New York, 1989.

Dunlop, James J., *Leading the Association: Striking the Right Balance Between Staff and Volunteers*, Foundation of the American Society of Association Executives, Washington, D.C., 1989.

Ernstthal, Henry, "Beyond UBIT: An Exploration," *Association, Management*, August 1988, American Society of Association Executives, Washington, D.C.

_____, "Some Thoughts on the Year 2000," *Leadership*, American Society of Association Executives, Washington, D.C., 1989.

Foundation of the American Society of Association Executives, *The Decision to Join: Insights Based on a Survey of Association Members and Nonmembers*, Washington, D.C., 1981.

_____, *Motivating Participation in Voluntary Membership Associations*, Washington, D.C., 1976.

Gallup Organization, *Poll on Volunteerism*, Princeton, New Jersey, 1986.

Jones, James R., "Customer Service Requires Entire Staff Support," *ASAE Membership Marketer*, July 1987, American Society of Association Executives, Washington, D.C.

Kilby, Dave, "Membership Retention" research paper, California Association of Chamber of Commerce Executives, Sacramento.

Kulczycki, Michael, Albert Sunseri, John Anderson, and Marsha Niebuhr, "Ensuring Success as a 'Member-Centered' Association: How to Use Market Research to Make Smarter Decisions," *A Sharing of Expertise & Experience*, Vol. 7, American Society of Association Executives, Washington, D.C. 1989.

Leepson, Evan, and Jill Zaklow, "Eliminating the Yawn Factor in Membership Literature," *A Sharing of Expertise & Experience*, Vol. 4, American Society of Association Executives, Washington, D,C., 1986.

Levin, Mark, "Turn Chapter/National Relations into a Win-Win Situation," *ASAE Membership Marketer*, August 1987, American Society of Association Executives, Washington, D.C.

Levitt, Theodore, *The Marketing Imagination*, The Free Press, New York, 1983.

Lovelock, Christopher H., *Services Marketing*, Prentice-Hall, Englewood Cliffs, New Jersey, 1984.

_____, and Charles B. Weinberg, *Marketing for Public and Nonprofit Managers*, John Wiley & Sons, New York, 1984.

McAdoo, Richard F., "Associations Must Develop a Needs-Driven Approach to Marketing," *Association Management*, September 1988, American Society of Association Executives, Washington, D.C.

_____, "Beyond Product Selling: An Integrated Approach to Association Marketing," *A Sharing of Expertise & Experience*, Vol. 7, American Society of Association Executives, Washington, D.C., 1989.

Meister, Miriam T., "Getting to Really Know Your Members," *A Sharing of Expertise & Experience*, Vol. 7, American Society of Association Executives, Washington, D.C., 1989.

_____, "Practical Association Research on a Shoestring Budget," *A Sharing of Expertise & Experience*, Vol. 6, American Society of Association Executives, Washington, D.C., 1988.

Milner, Neil, "One Hundred Ways to Generate Nondues Income," *Association Management*, August 1987, American Society of Association Executives, Washington, D.C.

Monroe, Kenneth E., Kathleen R. Lane, and Mark D. Johnson, "Who Needs You? Member Segmentation and Marketing Strategy," *A Sharing of Expertise & Experience*, Vol. 5, American Society of Association Executives, Washington, D.C., 1987.

Naisbitt, John, and Patricia Aburdene, *Megatrends 2000: The New Direction for the 1990s*, William Morrow and Company, Inc., New York, 1990.

Pritchard, Harmon O., Jr., "A Member's Lifetime Value," *Association Management*, June 1991, American Society of Association Executives, Washington, D.C.

Pitt, Leyland, "Pricing in Nonprofit Organizations," *Quarterly Review of Marketing* 12, No. 3, Spring 1987.

Pratt, Cynthia, "Increasing First-Anniversary Renewals," *Membership Recruitment and Retention*, American Society of Association Executives, Washington, D.C., 1986.

Schaefer, Mickey, "Chapter and National Play for the Same Team," *ASAE Membership Marketer*, August 1987, American Society of Association Executives, Washington, D.C.

Shark, Alan R., "Developing Strategic Marketing Planning and Monitoring System," *A Sharing of Expertise & Experience*, Vol. 7, American Society of Association Executives, Washington, D.C., 1989.

Sher, Debra, "Tracking Results of Membership Campaigns and Activities," *Membership Recruitment and Retention*, American Society of Association Executives, Washington, D.C., 1983.

Sirkin, Arlene Farber, "Getting the Edge," *Executive Update*, December 1989, Greater Washington Society of Association Executives, Washington, D.C.

_____, "Marketing the Product Line," *Marketing the Nonprofit Association*, Greater Washington Society of Association Executives, Washington, D.C., 1992.

_____, "Maximizing the Client-Researcher Partnership," *Marketing News*, October 1990.

_____, "No More Basket Cases," *Executive Update*, May 1991, Greater Washington Society of Association Executives, Washington, D.C.

Snyder, David Pearce, and Gregg Edwards, *Future Forces: An Association Executive's Guide to a Decade of Change and Choice*, Foundation of the American Society of Association Executives, Washington, D.C., 1984.

Spector, Robert, "New Strategic Plan Reverses 20-Year Membership Decline," *ASAE Membership Marketer*, November 1990, American Society of Association Executives, Washington, D.C.

Steinberg, Daniyel F., "Add a Personal Touch," *Association Management*, February 1985, American Society of Association Executives, Washington, D.C.

Washington Association Research Foundation, *A Bibliography of Association Management Literature*, George Washington University, Washington, D.C., 1990.

Zeithaml, Valarie A., A. Parasuraman, and Leonard L. Berry, *Delivering Quality Service: Balancing Customer Perceptions and Expectations*, Free Press, New York, 1990.